THE DEERHOLME VEGETABLE COOKBOOK

THE DEERHOLME
VEGETABLE
COOKBOOK

BILL JONES

TouchWood
Editions

This book is dedicated to my mother, Joan, and my father, Bill. Mom grew up in Nova Scotia on a diet of fish and potatoes; Dad had to teach her what vegetables were.

CONTENTS

RECITE LIST

PREFACE

haven't always loved vegetables. I recall shedding tears as a boy at the dinner table at the prospect of having to eat overcooked carrots in a family favorite called "the boiled dinner." To anyone growing up in Nova Scotia, this meant a big pot of broth loaded with onions, potatoes, cabbage, and carrots with a chunk of corned beef. To my young taste buds, it was an assault of strong flavors and mushy vegetables, and the peculiar funk that cabbage and carrots take on when they are boiled for hours revolted me. My family looked at me like I was crazy while they tucked into bowls of it. I preferred to pout and go hungry.

Little did I know that this would set me down the road to becoming a chef. Eventually I made a deal to make my own meal on "boiled dinner night," starting with peanut butter sandwiches and working my way up to pasta, salad, and stir-fries. My parents encouraged me, and soon I was cooking for the entire family and shifting the menu to things I enjoyed.

In my teens, I read a book called *Diet for a Small Planet*, which set off a whole new, and ultimately transformational, exploration of the world of vegetables and healthy cooking. Another watershed moment was the discovery of a book called *Moosewood Cookbook*. I was officially hooked on the excitement and power of vegetables. This even took me as far as a stint as a vegetarian in my twenties. That stint ended rather unceremoniously at a barbecue one weekend, when the smell of cooking ribs made me salivate and lose control. I had been living on a diet of brown rice, tofu, and vegetables for months and I was not only craving meat, I was craving excitement and variety. It seemed to me there had to be a way to balance these feelings and enjoy all aspects of our food culture. I have since taken the concept of balance with me into the kitchen, and it has served me well for many years.

There are many compelling reasons to add more vegetables to your plate. Health benefits, environmental sustainability, and economic impact are three good ones. In addition to these noble pursuits, however, flavor is always near the top of my list. For a while it seemed we were going in the wrong direction with the quality of vegetables available in our markets. That is still a disturbing trend, but one that has been countered by the parallel trend of a resurgence in great local products. Small farms are diversifying and bringing heirloom and well-grown vegetables to our markets. Farmers markets have returned with a vengeance and are popping up on every corner. Consumers are demanding better products year-round and the advancement of greenhouse technology has allowed us to produce decent products in a wide range of climates.

The history of vegetables is also a fascinating story of civilization itself. Many vegetables were first foraged in their native lands and then spread to the far corners of the globe. The spread was fuelled by our nomadic nature, commerce, and the desire to bring a little of the comforts of home to far-flung destinations. Central and South America were a treasure trove of vegetables that are commonplace in today's markets. Squash, green beans, corn, peppers, potatoes, and tomatoes are a few of the superstars that sprung from that region to dominate the diets of the world. Try to imagine Italian food without the tomato or Thai food without chili peppers. In historical terms, these are fairly recent additions that have been totally ingrained into the cuisines of those regions. That trend is simply continuing today as we introduce and grow more food from other lands in our local farms and gardens.

Much of my time as a chef is now taken up by the search for great ingredients, the cornerstone of all good cooking. Great ingredients are a key part of this book. You can find them in a local market, farmers market, grocery store, or your own garden. Vegetables, like most living things, usually begin to deteriorate the moment they are picked. How you treat, handle, and store them is critical to distilling the best from your produce. Moisture and oxygen are the main culprits, taking the produce on a journey into decay the moment the vegetable is harvested. This often means the best ingredients are found as close as possible to the dining table. Modern chefs take notice of this and have resurrected a movement called farm-to-table cooking that focuses on shortening the distances between our kitchens and our food sources. It also features some of the most exciting and delicious food out there.

Preservation is also key to great cooking. Traditional methods like fermenting, drying, and even aging have returned to the forefront of our cooking world. Freshness is a moment in time that does not linger. Preserving foods extends the season and often alters the flavor profile of foods as they undergo chemical alterations and become something deliciously and wildly different. New words like *kimchi* (salt- and spice-fermented vegetables) have entered our vocabulary, and the foods they described can easily be found in local pubs or food trucks parked at the side of the road.

Creativity is an important concept to me. A new direction often starts from an old idea viewed in a new way or from an altered perspective. All modern cooking embraces this in some form. Creativity is a product of fundamental ideas being assimilated and used to create a new product. At its heart, this book is really an exercise in creativity. It offers the fundamentals of working with vegetables and their properties as a foundation for putting a little excitement into your meals. I encourage you to take your favorite vegetables and experiment with different ways to prepare them. Take carrots: try making a pot of cabbage and carrot sauerkraut, roast some carrots with spices, or create carrot soups from a variety of ingredients. The days when recipes were passed down from generation to generation, based on what grew well locally and "what we always ate," are fading. The world is now a global village with Internet, TV, and social media helping to break the barriers that once constrained us. In my local store I can buy Thai seasonings, Spanish olives, and Persian delicacies. You probably can, too. Your idea of Sunday dinner might have influences from Italy, China, or the Middle East. Times have changed—and so should our idea of what to do with our vegetables.

This book is a love letter to vegetable cooking. It comes from a chef who has travelled the world eating and cooking, and now lives on a farm in the beautiful Cowichan Valley of Vancouver Island, British Columbia. It is the culmination of my journey so far in vegetable cooking. Recipes to me are only guidelines for great cooking. The techniques presented are the important part of making good food. This book presents a mix of traditional methods (like fire) combined with a few state-of-the-art flourishes. In essence, it is a celebration of the once humble vegetable and a new companion to exciting and satisfying cooking. Like most good concepts in life, it is a journey of discovery, not a destination.

Bill Jones
Deerholme Farm
Cowichan Valley, BC

ACKNOWLEDGMENTS

I'd like to thank the team at TouchWood for being so easy to work with and good at what they do. Head honcho Taryn Boyd is a fellow lover of books, and her passion is greatly appreciated; Pete Kohut, with his skill in design and love of Joy Division, has a unique approach that brings an edge into his art; Cailey Cavallin, a fine editor to work with, possesses expertise that transcends her tender age; Lesley Cameron's helpful editing suggestions made the manuscript a much better read; last but not least, I wish to extend a big thank you to publisher Pat Touchie, who sought me out here on the farm and helped coax three more books out of me.

On the home front, I owe a huge debt to my family and friends—particularly wifey, Lynn, and father-in-law, Ken—for the support (and kick in the pants) along the way. It takes many friends to get through life happily, and I am blessed with an abundance of willing and gullible companions.

Finally, a big hug and a scratch behind the ear to the farm canine Oliver, who is always photobombing the best pictures. He helps keep the squirrels on their toes and the deer on the perimeter of the gardens—at least while he's on duty and not sleeping!

INTRODUCTION

SOURCING

....

THE FOOD SYSTEM

When people refer to vegetables in a food system, they are really talking about the journey from the farm to your plate. The farm might be a greenhouse under an acre of glass or a bucolic farm surrounded by gentle hills and trees. Many people say the industrial farming model is broken, but that is only partially true. The system is constantly changing due to technology, economics, and customers' buying choices. Parts of the system have huge issues; industrial models often focus on profit and money-saving logistics ahead of flavor—or in some cases, ethics. But this is not always the case. Sometimes change is good, products improve over time, techniques become more efficient, and certain foods can even become more nutritious in the industrial model.

But at the same time, we can embrace local sources of food. The one truth we can't escape is that most foods (and their nutrients) begin to deteriorate the moment they are harvested. Just stand in a garden and taste a fresh tomato, pea, or carrot to realize the truth of that. Buying local food also supports people who live and work around you. Many do it for love and other noble ideals; few are in it for the money. When you buy local, you support your community and reap benefits in many delicious ways.

When choosing vegetables, it is useful to think of their path to the table. Whenever possible, you should eat the vegetables produced closest to you. It has been calculated that if everyone bought as little as ten percent of their total food purchases from local producers, the local economy would benefit massively. Not too many years ago, people would buy closer to 100 percent of their food from local producers. If people have access to good local food and the motivation to buy it, that figure of ten percent should be easily achievable.

WHERE DO YOU GET THE GOOD STUFF?

The best source of food is a garden you have planted and maintained. And it can save you a few dollars. Of course, not all of us have a plot of land to work. Sometimes the only option is to get food from people who can grow it for us (sometimes with far better results than we could achieve ourselves).

Transporting produce has always been a challenge for small farmers. Going to the farm gate is an excellent way to help farmers get their products to you. Other farms and businesses do the legwork for you. Programs like Community Supported Agriculture (CSA) source local vegetables and put together a selection for you each week. Usually you pay in advance for this service, giving the farmers seed money (literally) and reaping the rewards as the growing season progresses. Farmers markets are the next level up. Farmers gather at a convenient spot and set up tables displaying their handiwork. Shopping at the market is a good way to compare the different products and source some of the freshest food possible, sometimes only hours after harvest. It is also a great place to experience the community, get to know the farmers, meet friends, and generally enjoy life for a few hours.

Farmers markets happen weekly, but sometimes we need to go shopping every day of the week. A good local vegetable market is a great place to visit. I look for places that put up signs and are not afraid to tell you where the food comes from. I also look for a busy place that has a high turnover of products. I don't focus on organic perfection when I buy local, but I do look for signs of age and abuse (blemishes and bruises) on products to judge their freshness.

And yes, sometimes I go to the big box stores. We all need a bit of convenience at times, and if I'm off looking for large quantities of olive oil or light bulbs, I might pick up something nice in the produce section (local or otherwise). Sometimes you just need variety, and a coconut and pineapple curry fits the bill perfectly. Life should be about enjoyment at the core—stress is bad for you, so why stress out over the odd trip down the global food system path?

STORAGE MATTERS

If we accept that most food begins to deteriorate the moment it is picked, knowing the basic physical and chemical properties of food can help us slow the decay. The primer on vegetables that follows looks at some of the specific qualities of plants that affect their storage potential. It can all be distilled down to a few general rules:

1. Vegetables with higher water contents are generally more perishable.
2. Green leafy vegetables are high in water content and best eaten shortly after harvest. Some delicate greens are now sold in nitrogen flushed packs to prolong their shelf life and slow down the decay process.
3. Dense vegetables, like squash, potatoes, onions, beets, cabbage, and carrots, usually store well due to a high starch content, tightly packed leaf structure, or high sugar content (like beets and carrots).
4. All vegetables should be processed as soon as possible to preserve maximum nutritional benefits.

When you come back from the garden or market, you have to perform a kind of triage on your produce, separating out some items for quick consumption and storing others. Some items prefer dry storage, and others like cool temperatures; some can be pickled, dehydrated, and frozen, while others like to be refreshed in cold water to plump them up and restore some of their vigor. So read on, ignite your curiosity, and don't be afraid to try something new—it might surprise you.

FRESH VEGETABLE PRIMER

We eat many types of plants. Starting from below ground, we find roots, tubers, bulbs, corms, and rhizomes. Above ground, we find edible new shoots, stems, stocks, leaves, seedpods, and seeds. How you handle these depends on many factors, including their composition of sugars, starches, and fibres. Below is an overview of locally available produce with some information about their individual characteristics.

ROOT VEGETABLES

To understand vegetables, it helps to look at their designated role in nature. Many of our root vegetables are tuberous roots or tap roots. They are primarily storage organs for energy for the plant and help to anchor it in the soil. The energy is stored in the form of carbohydrates. Of particular importance are the roots that store carbohydrates in the form of starch. Biologists distinguish true roots such as tuberous roots and taproots from non-roots such as tubers, rhizomes, corms, and bulbs, though some, like celeriac, contain both taproot and hypocotyl (stem) tissues. In general, the starchy qualities lead us to treat most root vegetables in similar fashions, with some modifications to allow for the type and quantity of starch they contain. It is interesting to note that root vegetables where the energy is stored as starches have been coveted as food sources since the dawn of humans, for both their ability to provide nutrition and quick energy and their ease of cultivation, cooking, and storage.

Beets (*Beta vulgaris ssp.*)

The beetroot is a true taproot of the beet plant. The leaves are edible and excellent when young and fresh. Mature beetroots are very dense, but can still be eaten raw if grated. Generally, beets are cooked before eating and can be boiled, steamed, roasted, or grilled. Once tender, the beet can be made into salads, pickled, and puréed.

The history of beets is a little murky, but it's believed the plant originated around the shores of the Mediterranean Sea. There is also historical evidence placing it in the Persian and Indian regions. Originally it was more of a mass of tops with small yellowish roots, similar to today's Swiss chard. It was selectively bred over centuries to produce the multicolored, sweet roots we see today. Breeders are continually producing new varieties, including red, white, yellow, and variegated varieties.

Beets keep well for long periods of time. Choose beets that are plump, heavy, and blemish-free. Wrinkled skin is a sign of dehydration, generally from advanced age. Beetroot is an excellent source of sugars, nutrients, and minerals, particularly manganese. Betanin gives the beet its deep red color. Although it is not completely broken down in the body, it is eliminated harmlessly and colorfully. What is absorbed is thought to help safeguard the body from certain vascular (blood system) issues.

Beets are relatively easy to cultivate and usually need 55 to 65 days from germination to harvest of the root. The greens are available for harvest in about half that time. Some of my favorite varieties are Bulls Blood (deep red), Detroit Dark Red, Early Wonder (red heirloom), Golden Beet (deep yellow), and Chiogga (variegated).

Carrots (*Daucus carota subsp. sativus*)

Carrots are a true taproot and although usually orange in color, purple, red, white, yellow, and multicolored varieties are available in the market, with more variants coming each season. The modern carrot is sweet and crisp with a mild taste. It was domesticated from the wild carrot, believed to have originated in Persia but now found all over the world. The wild carrot has large foliage and sports a woody and bitter taproot. The domesticated carrot is now one of the world's most popular vegetables, and is eaten both raw and cooked in many cuisines.

When first cultivated, carrots were grown for their aromatic leaves (used as a flavoring herb) and seeds rather than their roots. Selective breeding has sweetened and tenderized the root to produce a sweet (almost five percent sugar) vegetable that is rich in nutrients, dietary fibres, and energy. Carrots are loaded with carotenes, vitamins, and phytonutrients. Two carotenoid compounds, lutein and zeaxanthin, have been implicated in helping reduce the effects of ultraviolet radiation absorption in the eyes, helping keep our vison in good shape as we age. Cooking carrots helps release almost ten times more carotene than you would obtain from raw carrots.

The greens of the plant are edible, but should only be harvested from young plants. The mature leaves develop toxic alkaloids and concentrate nitrates from the soil. It is probably all right to eat them in small doses, but people sensitive to nitrates should be cautious.

There are four general types of carrots, categorized by shape. Long carrots such as the Imperator are the most commonly found carrot in our markets. Medium carrots include cultivars like the Nante and Chantenay varieties. This category also contains many of the colored varieties, including Belgian White, Cosmic Purple, and Yellowstone. Ball carrots are a type bred for their unique round shape and include varieties like Thumbelina and Paris Market. The final variety is mini carrots, grown for their small, perfect form and crisp, light flavor. My favorite varieties include Short and Sweet, Babette, Mignon, and Little Finger.

Celeriac (*Apium graveolens var. rapaceum*)

Also called celery root, celeriac is a popular vegetable native to Europe and the Mediterranean. It has a bulbous hypocotyl (stem), below which the root system continues downward. The flesh is starchy and mild, a cross between potato and mild celery. The flesh is eaten raw, shredded in salads, cooked into chunks, or mashed to make excellent purées and soups.

Celeriac is a temperamental vegetable to grow, and it needs a lot of nutrients and care to develop into a large specimen. It takes a long time to mature, over 100 days in my region. Like many root vegetables, it benefits from a little frost to develop flavor and sweetness. Diamante is the cultivar most widely planted, but other fine varieties are Monarch and Prinz.

When preparing celeriac it is common to peel the vegetable into water acidulated with lemon juice, vinegar, or vitamin C powder. This prevents the flesh from oxidizing and turning an unpleasant shade of grey.

Parsnips (*Pastinaca sativa*)

Closely related to the carrot and parsley, parsnips were cultivated from the wild plants of Eurasia. The flesh can be eaten raw or cooked, and is an excellent source of vitamins and minerals. It is also a great source of dietary fibre. Parsnips are particularly good roasted, as the high sugar content produces a nutty, caramelized flavor.

Parsnips are relatively easy to grow, and mature in about 120 days. You can over-winter parsnips by covering them with a thick layer of mulch. Parsnips are biannual, so they will continue to grow in the spring. It is best to harvest before this stage as the roots tend to become tough and bitter. Some of my favorite varieties include Gladiator and Javelin, which are both hearty and disease resistant in my region.

Radishes (*Raphanus sativus*)
Radishes are annual or biennial crops grown for their swollen tap-roots. The shape can be rounded, tapering, or cylindrical. The skin color ranges from white, pink, red, purple, yellow, and green to black; the flesh is usually white, but reddish, blush, and variegated (Watermelon radishes) are available in the market.

Smaller spring or summer types have rounded or tapered roots that are sweet and crisp when fresh. Larger winter radishes can be quite large (up to 2 feet / 60 cm) in size, and include the famous daikon root, developed in China but commonly known by its Japanese name. All radishes become bitter and tough if left in the ground for too long.

The humble radish is a fine early example of a plant that was taken from the wild and spread all over the planet. It is believed to have originated in Southeast Asia, where scientists have traced the purest forms of wild plants. The Greeks and Romans were very fond of radishes and spread the plant around their empires. It also appears to be one of the first European foods to have been introduced to North America.

A round, red-skinned type called Cherry Belle is the variety most often seen in our markets. My favorites include French Breakfast (elongated with a white tip), White Icicle (white tapered root), Amethyst (purple), Starburst (watermelon type: white with red interior), Black Spanish Round (black skin and spicy flesh), and Altaglobe (an easy-to-grow and delicious red variety). Most of these types are eaten raw, but occasionally they are added to braises and stews.

Daikon refers to a whole range of large, cylindrical, white radishes originally from Asia. Some varieties, like Sakurajima, are spicy-hot; others, like the Masato, are mild and juicy. Daikon is often eaten raw, pickled, and cooked in a wide array of recipes.

Turnips (*Brassica rapa sp.*) and Rutabaga (*Brassica napus sp.*)
Turnips and rutabaga are similar plants with a bulbous taproot. Turnips were one of the main crops in the temperate regions of Europe, a mainstay root vegetable crop well before the introduction of the potato. The leaves are also edible and usually called turnip greens. The rutabaga, thought to be a cross between turnip

and cabbage plants, may have originated in Scandinavia or Russia. Occasionally the labelling is not clear in markets and turnips and rutabaga are mislabelled as each other. The *Brassica rapa* family also has many members that are grown exclusively for the leaves, including mustards, mizuna, napa cabbage, and rapini.

Turnip's root is high in vitamin C and is a good source of a variety of vitamins and minerals. The greens are even more nutritious and are an excellent source of vitamins A, C, and K, folate, and calcium. The greens are also high in lutein. Turnips and rutabagas are fairly easy to grow—just remember to eat those greens! The turnip is often harvested as a young vegetable. My favorite varieties include a number of colorful globes such as the white Hakurei, the yellow Golden Ball, and the classic Purple Topped White Globe. Rutabagas to look for include Laurentian, Joan, and an heirloom French variety called Collet Vert.

TUBERS

Tubers are a variety of modified plant structures that have been enlarged to store energy for the plant to get through the winter months or times of hardship (drought, etc.), and as a vehicle for reproduction of the plant. Some of these roots are fairly perishable. Potatoes are an example of a stem tuber that grows as a stolon or an offshoot of the plant's root system. Sweet potatoes are an example of a root tuber that forms as a bulge in the root system and is enlarged to store energy. This energy is stored as carbohydrate in the form of starch.

Jerusalem Artichoke (*Helianthus tuberosus*) and
Crosne (*Stachys affinis*)
These rhizomes come from two different species, but they look similar. The Jerusalem artichoke is a species of sunflower native to eastern North America, and is also called the sunchoke. The plant was cultivated by First Nations cultures and was introduced to the first settlers who then introduced it to Europe and the rest of the world.

The Jerusalem artichoke contains about ten percent protein and very little starch, and is a rich source of the carbohydrate inulin, which is a preform of fructose. When stored, the tuber converts inulin into fructose, giving it a sweet taste. Inulin is also used as an important source of dietary fibre in many commercially manufactured food products. It cannot be broken down by the body. If you eat a lot of it, you might experience gas, and in some cases gastric pain.

The effects are lessened if the tubers are aged properly (stored for several weeks) and cooked before eating.

Crosne is also called the Chinese artichoke and is a member of the herbaceous *Lamiaceae* family (related to the mints and dead nettles). The rhizome of the plant is interesting to look at—it looks like the vegetable equivalent of a larva—and has a mild and nutty flavor. Crosne are fairly easy to grow and just need to be well watered and fed occasionally. The tubers are harvested when the plants leaves die off. The tubers must be removed from the ground and washed and brushed before use. If left in the ground, they will wither and become bitter. There are cream and red varieties of the rhizome available.

Both plants are easy to grow. In fact, one issue with the plant is confining its growth. Raised (or isolated) beds are usually recommended. The plants can be grown from the previous year's crop and will reproduce in abundance.

Potatoes (*Solanum tuberosum*)

The potato is a starchy, tuberous crop from a perennial nightshade. The plant is native to the Andes region, but it has become a key part of the world's food supply. About 200 wild potato species occur throughout Central and South America, and there are believed to be about 5,000 cultivated potato varieties. Cross-breeding occurs often, and potatoes can transfer qualities between the various species. Most potatoes are defined by the type of starch they contain. High-starch potatoes like the russet are great for mashing, baking, and frying. Low-starch potatoes are often called waxy and are great for boiling, baking, and using in salads. There is, however, lots of overlap; many potatoes have starch properties that fall in the middle of these two extremes.

The storage of potatoes is critical to preserving their starch content. The long-term storage area must be dark and with a constant temperature around 39°F (5°C) to help to slow the natural deterioration of the potato. At this optimum temperature, the potato can be stored for up to a year. Temperatures below this level cause the starch to convert to sugar. This alters the taste of the potato, and leads to the production of compounds like acrylamides, which are linked to carcinogenic concerns and may pose a long-term health risk. When exposed to sunlight, potatoes produce chlorophyll and turn green. The green is harmless, but it indicates that the potato has started to activate toxic compounds (solanine and chaconine) that form part of the potato's natural defence mechanism. It is best to cut off any

green flesh or even discard the potato. Solanine is also water- and fat-soluble, so boiling or frying will reduce its concentrations.

Potatoes are among the easiest crops to grow and often volunteer in the garden if you manage to miss a few potatoes in previous harvests. There are many varieties to explore, but I like a variety of shapes and colors in the garden. Russets are a great storing and baking potato, Chieftain is a fine red-skinned variety, Russian Banana fingerlings are small and delicious roasting potatoes, Purple Peruvian are a fine purple fingerling, German Butterball is a delicious yellow variety, and Kennebec is an outstanding white potato for all-around use.

Sweet Potatoes (*Ipomoea batatas*)

The sweet potato is one of the most nutritious vegetables out there. In North America, they are often labelled yams in markets. True yams are tropical and semi-tropical vegetables that have a greyish-white, starchy flesh. The sweet potato is a large and starchy tuberous root with a sweet flavor and widely varying shades of flesh. The edible tuberous root is long and tapered, with a smooth skin whose color ranges between yellow, orange, red, brown, purple, and beige. Its flesh color ranges from beige through white, red, pink, violet, yellow, orange, and purple. It is believed to have originated in Central or South America.

Sweet potatoes require a bit of care to grow in northern climates because they are a tropical plant. For example, they need a black plastic soil covering to let them absorb as much heat as possible from the sun. They also need a loose sandy soil with lots of nutrients. I have had good luck with a varietal called Georgia Jet; Beauregard is another tasty cool-climate variety. Recommended white varieties include the Frazier White and the O'Henry. Most of the commercially available sweet potatoes in the local markets are two main varieties, Jewell and Garnet, from the southern US states. Once harvested, the sweet potato must be held in a warm area like a cupboard for about ten days to cure. This greatly adds to the sweetness and moisture content of the root. The cured yam can be stored in a root cellar or basement for several months. Over the first couple of months the flavor will continue to improve; it will then remain stable for several more months.

Sweet potatoes with dark orange flesh have higher levels of beta-carotene and tend to be moister and sweeter than the pale-flesh varieties. They are all a rich source of complex carbohydrates, dietary fibre, vitamins, and micronutrients. Most of the micronutrients become more available for absorption by the body once the root has been cooked, particularly by dry methods such as roasting. The sweet potato ranks as one of the most nutritious vegetables available to us.

....

STALKS AND SHOOTS

Most plants are tender when they first shoot up from the ground. As they grow and age, plants develop fibres for strength and use some of their stored energy to toughen up against the forces of nature swirling around them. Timing of the harvest is often designed to take advantage of the peak edibility of the plant.

Asparagus (*Asparagus officinalis*)

Asparagus is a spring vegetable and widely cultivated as a vegetable crop. The plant is thought to have originated in the Mediterranean region and then been exported to many parts of the planet. Grown as a vegetable and as a medicinal herb—reputed to combat fatigue— it was a favorite of the Romans, and was spread through Europe during the expansion of their empire. The young shoots are eaten before the buds start to open. Once the buds open and begin to shoot out ferns, the plant becomes woody and bitter. The stem thickness indicates the age of the plant. Shoots from new plants are tender and thicken as the plant ages. It takes two to three years for new plants to produce larger spears, which increase in size as the plant ages.

Asparagus is a good source of many nutrients, including vitamins C, K, and E. It is an excellent source of dietary fibre and is rich in minerals. It is also rich in an amino acid called asparagine, which is thought to be helpful in maintaining healthy brain functions.

Most asparagus shoots are green, although some are a lovely shade of purple. The purple spears have a slightly higher sugar content and slightly fewer fibres, making them very tender. The color comes from the presence of higher levels of anthocyanin (a powerful antioxidant); it fades to deep green when cooked thoroughly, so lighter cooking is advised. White asparagus is the result of blanching (covering in mulch) to keep the spears away from sunshine and from developing color from chlorophyll development. The result is a creamy white spear that is delicate and sweet, with a slightly nutty taste.

Asparagus is usually planted from crowns (root clusters) in the early spring. It takes a couple of years to establish, but can be long-lived, particularly if you plant fungus-resistant varieties like Mary

Washington or Jersey Knight. Guelph Millennium is a purple-tipped variety that is fairly cold- and frost-resistant. Sweet Purple is the recommended choice for asparagus with full purple tips and stalks.

Celery (*Apium graveolens var. dulce*)

Celery is believed to have originated in the Mediterranean region and was originally coveted for its seeds, which were believed to have great medicinal properties. The seeds contain an essential oil called apiol that is good only in small doses: high concentrations can cause liver and kidney issues. Over the years, the plant was cultivated to produce long, straight stems. The stem was originally hollow and has been selectively bred to produce the solid, crisp stalks we see today.

The leaves are strongly flavored and are great to add to stocks and soups. Celery can be eaten raw, pickled, and cooked as a vegetable. Rich in antioxidants, it has been shown to have anti-inflammatory properties. It is also rich in vitamin C and a great source of dietary fibre. Steaming is the best way to cook and preserve its nutrients. Celery is a key part of mirepoix (chopped onion, celery, and carrot), the starting point of many recipes.

There are many types of cultivars usually categorized under green (sometimes called Pascal) and red (such as Redventure) varieties. Most commercial production is of the Pascal type. Celery is a relatively high-maintenance vegetable. Most of the commercial growers use a lot of chemicals to keep it healthy, and some of those chemicals remain in the vegetable as residue, making organic celery a much better option.

Celery is a heavy feeding plant and requires constant moisture. It is a good idea to make a trench beside the plant to continually supply it with water in the hot days of summer. Cold weather will cause the plant to bolt and produce seeds, so covering it in mulch and row covers in the cool evenings is a good idea. Recommended varieties include the hearty Victoria and the tender and early-ripening Tango.

Chard (*Beta vulgaris subsp. cicla*)

Chard (often called Swiss chard or occasionally silverbeet) originated in the Mediterranean Basin and was an oceanside plant. The wild plant is known as sea beet. The leaves are large and reddish or green; the stems come in a variety of colors. The plant is highly nutritious and contains a wide range of vitamins, minerals, and antioxidants. It is particularly high in vitamins A, K, and C. Chard contains a number of compounds called flavonoids that are reputed to have heart-protecting properties and help balance the absorption of sugars in the blood.

Chard is one vegetable that is hardy in the garden but deteriorates quickly after harvest. It is tastiest when young and crisp, but also tasty in the middle of its growth cycle. Luckily, it is a variety that can be continually harvested and might produce two to three crops before it bolts. When the plant is near the end of its prime cycle, the stalks toughen and become very stringy in texture. The plant also contains oxalic acid, an organic crystal that irritates the urinary tract and is linked to the formation of kidney stones. The crystals become larger as the plant ages—another reason to eat only young stems and leaves.

Chard is fairly easy to cultivate, and it does well in our coastal climates. It favors cooler nights and colder weather and often over-winters in my garden. Many cultivars work well in our region. I like the Fordhook Giant for green chard, Rhubarb for red, and Eldorado for yellow. Multicolor plants like Bright Lights (red, yellow, and white) are visually stunning and tasty.

Fennel (*Foeniculum vulgare*)

Fennel is a perennial herb that is grown as both an herb and a veg-etable. The vegetable version is sometimes called Florence Fennel, and its swollen stalk is harvested. The base is often called a bulb, but it is more correctly a bulb-like stem. The plant originated in the Mediterranean region but has spread to many parts of the world, thriving on sea coasts and near water in general.

The leaves and stalk are highly aromatic with a subtle liquorice scent. That aroma comes from a compound called anethole, also found in anise and star anise. It also lends the fennel a sweetness that is far more potent than an equal amount of sugar. It has reputed antibacterial and antifungal properties, as well as properties that aid digestion. It is used in many cultures as a digestive aide.

Herb fennel is ridiculously easy to grow and often spreads around the garden. Bulb fennel is usually started in the greenhouse and transplanted to the garden when the soil warms up. It is a fairly low-maintenance plant once it is in the ground. Favorite varieties are Selma Fino (flat bulb) and Finale (round bulb). Both produce crisp white bulbs with excellent flavor.

Fresh fennel is pure white and free of blemishes. As it ages, it tends to brown; the outer leaves will dehydrate and should be trimmed. I cut off any brown spots and use the outer leaves for making vegetarian stocks. It is best to use up fennel in the week fol-lowing harvest. The leaves and stem shoots will deteriorate first and should be removed and stored separately. I stand them in a container of water to prolong the shelf life for a few days.

Kohlrabi (*Brassica oleracea Gongylodes group*)
Kohlrabi is a vegetable that does not get a lot of loving here in North America. In Europe it is popular in the Germanic cultures. The plant's origins are a little murky, but it's believed to have evolved as a cross between two brassica cousins, cabbage and turnip. The flavor is crisp, a bit like broccoli stem crossed with a little bite of radish. The edible portion is actually a swollen stem that grows above ground and gives the kohlrabi its strange shape. Both the stem and leaves are edible. The leaves have a flavor similar to that of collard greens or kale.

Kohlrabi is packed with antioxidants and is a good source of vitamins C and B6, calcium, and potassium as well as dietary fibre. It has many phytonutrients, such as isothiocyanates, which are associated with anti-inflammatory and anticancer properties. The flesh makes a great pickle and can be roasted whole and peeled to intensify the flavors.

Kohlrabi, an easy plant to grow, is eaten raw, pickled, or cooked. The stem ball has a layer of fibre that can be tolerated in younger specimens, but is inedible in older stems. The fibrous layer is thick, and it is usually removed with a paring knife before eating. One of the main cultivars is called Gigante (also called Superschmelz), which forms large, uniform vegetables. The plant will happily overwinter in the coastal garden, and once picked will keep for another month with little drop-off in texture or flavor. Kohlrabi also comes in smaller, tender, green and purple varieties. The purple versions (such as Kolibri) are beautiful to look at, but once peeled for eating they resemble the other varieties—which all have creamy-white flesh.

BULB VEGETABLES
Bulb vegetables are aromatic vegetables that add flavor to a wide variety of dishes. Garlic, chives, spring onions, shallots, and a range of onions and leeks are all part of this family. Usually they are the flesh base of the stem that has grown in concentric layers. Garlic forms into individual cloves under the covering layers. Usually the bulb is the prize with the plants, but some variants have been developed to make the leaves above ground tender and delicious—like chives and green onions. The entire family, particularly the garlic bulb, is renowned for its medicinal properties.

Chives (*Allium schoenoprasum*)
Chives are the smallest member of the bulb family. Commonly distributed around the world, the plant is native to Asia, Europe,

and North America. Chives are usually eaten raw as an herb. The edible portion is the scape that rises above the roots. The plant also sends up a woody stem that bears the seed head. This portion is usually removed as it is extremely fibrous. The flower and seeds are also edible.

Garlic chives (*Allium tuberosum*) originated in China and India. They are robust-growing chives with a somewhat flattened scape. Their flavor is an unusual combination of chive, garlic, and floral. These chives are used in many Chinese and Indian dishes, where both the stems and flower heads are used.

The medicinal properties of chives hinge on the presence of organic sulphur compounds that have stimulant, antiseptic, and diuretic properties. These qualities are similar to those of garlic, but in far smaller quantities. Chives are rich in vitamins A and C, calcium, and iron.

Chives are easy to grow and are very low-maintenance plants. They do well in containers and can brighten up a patio or windowsill. The plant has insect-repelling properties and so should be spread around the garden—something it will happily do on its own. It is easy to grow and self-seed once established. You usually don't see a lot of chive varieties on the market and will often find only one variety: "common" chives. You may also come across a giant variant called Siberian Giant Chives (*Allium ledebourianum*). Garlic chives come in the common variety and a flat-stemmed variant called Lions Mane. Many wild onions are used mainly for the leaves, including Pacific Northwest native onions like the Nodding Onion (*Allium cernuum*).

Garlic (*Allium sativum sp.*)

The history of garlic goes way back in the story of civilization. It is believed to have been native to central Asia before being transported everywhere humans live. It has taken a prominent position in every society in which it has been introduced—as both a food and a medicine.

There are two main subspecies of garlic, hardneck and softneck. There are hundreds of cultivars available on the market. Softneck garlics thrive in warmer climates and are generally the garlic you find in most stores (usually a subspecies called artichoke). They mature rapidly and have excellent storage properties. Hardneck garlic is a good hearty choice for northern climates and there is a lot of diversity in the types, with mild, spicy, large, and small clove variants.

All garlics are easy to grow and can be planted in the fall for early harvest in the growing season. You can also plant in spring for a later harvest. The plant is reproduced asexually, with cloves from a previous year put back in the ground the following season. Hardneck garlic produces a scape that is cut off and used as a vegetable. This diverts more energy into producing a large and intensely flavored bulb.

Garlic can be stored at a warm temperature for many weeks with no effect on quality. Eventually the clove will begin to sprout and produce a green shoot. Commercially, garlic is stored at very cold conditions to delay this process. It will also keep longer if the tops are attached; traditionally, these tops were braided and hung together for storage.

Garlic is rich in vitamins, particularly B6 and C, and minerals, particularly manganese, but we eat garlic in such small quantities that this is usually a negligible source of these in our diets. Garlic has intense antiseptic (from allicin) and antifungal (from phytocide) properties, and produces many complex sulphur compounds and a protective substance called allixin, both of which are thought to have to immune system-boosting and anticancer properties.

Leeks (*Allium ampeloprasum var. porrum*)

The leek is a member of the allium family that is cultivated for the lower portion of leaf sheaths that is neither a stem nor a stalk. Rather than forming a bulb, the leek develops a long cylinder of translucent layers. Soil is pushed up to blanch the stem and create a more edible surface. The leek originated in Central Asia and spread quickly around the world, becoming a staple in ancient Egypt before moving on to the rest of the planet.

The white flesh is usually valued more than the green leaf; it is mild and cooks to a very tender texture. The leaf can be added to stocks and soups. Leeks contain similar sulphur compounds to garlic, but in much lower quantities. They are rich in antioxidants and vitamins, particularly folic acid and vitamin A, and contain several essential minerals, particularly iron and magnesium.

There are two main variants: smaller summer types and larger overwinter leeks. The plant is often started from seed in a flat then transplanted to the garden as the soil warms up. Once established, the leek grows to hardy maturity. Overwintered varieties will last through the cold season and can be harvested in the spring as needed. Good summer types include Lancia and Varna. Great overwintering leeks include Lancelot, Bandit, and Lexton varieties.

Bulb Onions (*Allium cepa*)

Sometimes called the common onion, this vegetable could probably justify having an entire book of its own. Onion species are found all over the planet, though their origin at this point is a little murky. The onion basically has been successful everywhere. Most of the onions we see today are products of cultivation and breeding to develop specific characteristics like size, shape, color, and sweetness. It has also always been very good at both escaping and adapting to the conditions around it.

The onion plant has a fan of hollow, bluish-green leaves that usually produces a bulb at the base. Some varieties, like the shallot and the rarer potato onion, produce a cluster of bulb. Onions are an integral part of cuisines in most parts of the world. They are eaten raw, pickled, roasted, and sautéed in a wide range of dishes. The bulb is an energy storage system for the plant.

Onions are usually broken down into three types based on color: yellow, red, and white. Yellow onions are the dominant onion found in the markets and are strong-flavored with an excellent shelf life. Red onions are milder and more perishable. White onions are mild and often called sweet, and have both a higher sugar content and the shortest storage life. In addition to color, onions have been bred for size (for example, pearl onions or cippolini).

The levels of most essential nutrients in onions are fairly low, but they bring about four percent sugar and a number of phytochemical compounds to the table. All varieties are good sources of vitamin C, calcium, and iron. Red onions are a little higher in fibre; both red and yellow onions have higher flavonoid contents linked to anti-inflammatory and health-promoting properties. All have a complex blend of healthy sulphur compounds similar to garlic. Sulphenic acid is released when onions are chopped. This is what causes our eyes to sting, bringing on the tears. Turning on an exhaust fan while you chop will help lessen the sting.

Onions are heavy-feeding crops and need a good level of nutrients in the soil. I feed the soil with compost and keep the area well drained. Onions can be grown from fresh seed or from sets. The plant needs a great deal of water as the roots are fairly shallow. It is harvested when the leaves die back; they can be pulled and left in the field to dry for a couple of days before being stored in a well-ventilated, cool storage space. The shelf life will vary based on the moisture and sugar content of the onions. The higher these factors, the shorter the shelf life. Sweet white onions should ideally be used as soon as possible—within a couple of days for best results. They can also be refrigerated for up to a month.

Yellow onions make up the bulk of onions used in North America. Often producers and retailers do not differentiate between breeds. Patterson is a good, hearty, long-lasting variety, Cortland is another famous varietal. Red onions are next in popularity with Ruby Ring and Red Zeppelin (my all-time favorite onion name) making good choices. White onions are divided into sweet onion—with famous names like Walla Walla, Vidalia, and Maui onions leading the group—and white storage onions—for example, White Wing and Sierra Blanca. Shallots are bunching onions that are easy to grow. I've had good results with varietals like Ambition and the classic French Red. We grow many other types of fresh green onions such as Japanese Kincho, Ramrod Scallions, Egyptian/Welsh (*Allium fistulosum*), and native onions like Nodding Onion and Ramps (*Allium tricoccum*). So many onions, so little time!

FRUIT VEGETABLES

Fruit vegetables are those that technically come under the classification of fruits and vegetables. A prime example is the tomato, which is a "fruit" by scientific means as it is developed from the ovary in the base of a flower as in the case of any other fruit. From a legal and culinary perspective, however, they are "vegetables." Peppers, beans, eggplant, and squash are also fruits. Go figure.

Beans (*Fabaceae sp.*)

"Bean" is a common name for large edible plant seeds of several species in the family *Fabaceae*. The term originally referred to the broad or fava bean family, but was later expanded to include common (*Phaseolus vulgaris*) beans (like black, kidney, pinto, and navy) and runner beans (like Scarlet Emperor), vigna beans (like adzuki and mung), and many other related plants such as soybeans, peas, and chickpeas (garbanzos).

Snap (or green) beans (see below) in the market are unripe cultivars of the common bean that have been selectively grown for the sweetness and tenderness of the pod. The entire bean family is huge, with more than 17,000 varieties documented. The plant names are confusing and often mean different things in different parts of the world. With such a convoluted picture, there are different origins for bean types around the world. Some types, like fava, soybeans, and chickpeas, are believed to have originated in central Asia. Many modern bean varieties originated in Central and South America.

Beans have significant amounts of fibre and soluble fibre, with 1 cup (250 mL) of cooked beans providing 9–13 grams of fibre. Beans are also high in protein, complex carbohydrates, folate, and iron. Raw, dried beans contain high concentrations of lectin (a natural plant defence mechanism) that is toxic raw, therefore most dried beans should be cooked before eating. It takes a lot of real estate to grow a useable crop, so we tend to get most of our beans from larger local suppliers and concentrate on growing beans with edible pods and peas.

Snap/Green Beans (*Phaseolus vulgaris*)

Snap beans—also known as green beans, haricots verts, filet, or string beans—are the unripe fruit of various cultivars of the common bean. They are eaten fresh or pickled, and can be frozen. Most varieties are green, but yellow, white, purple, red, black, and mottled versions have been developed.

Snap beans are a rich source of vitamins K, A, and the B complex. They are also extremely good sources of antioxidants and carotenoids, and contain a good range of minerals, including manganese and silicon, along with health-promoting dietary fibres.

Snap beans are divided in two major groups based on growing habit: bush beans and pole beans. Bush beans are short, self-supporting plants, around 2 feet (66 cm) tall. Pole beans are climbing vines and require support from a trestle or wire to grow upright. There are over 100 varieties of snap beans available, with many similar products coming from the bush and pole varietals.

Recommended bush beans are Jade (green), Royal Burgundy (purple), Carson (yellow), and Dragon's Tongue (mottled white and purple). Recommended pole beans are Fortex Filet (green), Kentucky Wonder Wax (yellow), and Musica (green Romano [flat] type).

Sweet Peas (*Pisum sativum*)

The sweet pea is an edible seed or seedpod, and is botanically a fruit. The wild pea originated in the Mediterranean Basin and parts of the Middle East. The name "pea" is also used to describe other edible seeds, such as the pigeon pea (*Cajanus cajan*) and the cowpea (*Vigna unguiculata*). The sweet pea is an annual plant and a cool season crop. The immature seedpods are eaten and many varieties (like snow peas) have been developed to focus on producing sweet and tender pods. Seedpods are usually eaten fresh—in fact, sweet seed varieties (like the English pea) are *best* eaten fresh; large quantities are consumed as frozen products.

Sweet peas are sweet and starchy, but high in fibre; protein; vitamins K, B complex, and C; and minerals like phosphorus, magnesium, copper, iron, and zinc. They are also rich in phytonutrients such as lutein and coumestrol (reputed to show promise in fighting some forms of stomach cancer). Other interesting components are saponins, believed to be powerful antioxidants with anti-inflammatory properties.

There are many cultivars in the sweet pea family with both bush and pole varieties. The pod color varies from green to yellow and purple, and the types are usually grouped into shelling, sugar snap, and snow pea varieties. Recommended shelling varieties are Green Arrow, Mr. Big, and Purple Mist (with an edible purple pod). The best snap varieties are Cascadia and Sugar Daddy. Our best snow pea is the dependable Oregon Sugar Pod II—and for something different, a yellow variety called Golden.

Cucumbers (*Cucumis sativus*)

The cucumber is the fruit of a creeping vine that originated in South Asia, probably India. Originally cucumbers were very bitter, but this trait has been selectively bred from the plant. Modern varieties have been adapted to grow in seedless (or near seedless) varieties (sometimes called burpless) that create fruit without pollination—for example, hybrid English or Persian varieties.

Most garden cultivars have seeds and require pollination. Bees are critical to the commercial production of field cucumbers, as many of the plants need pollen from a different plant to form fruit. Cucumbers grown to eat fresh are called slicing cucumbers. They are mainly eaten in the unripe green form, as the mature yellow fruit becomes increasingly bitter. We grow relatively few varieties here compared to India, where there are many varietals used for cooking and pickling. In general, cucumbers here are grouped into seeded field (like Olympian and Dasher), English (like Tasty Green and Roxynante), Persian (like Sultan and Green Fingers), pickling (like Excelsior and Harmonie), and heirloom types (like Lemon or Crystal Apple). Cucumbers do not store well and should be used soon after picking or preserved as pickles.

Eggplant (*Solanum melongena*)

Eggplant is a member of the nightshade family and is related to both tomatoes and potatoes. Believed to have originated in Southeast Asia and India, the fruit is botanically classed as a berry and contains edible seeds. The leaves and stems are considered toxic due to the presence of solanine (similar to potatoes). The fruit was originally white and egg-shaped, hence the name. The fruit has a long history of use in the Middle East, long before it was introduced to Europe. Today we see eggplant grown all over the world in a variety of purple, pink, white, and mottled colors and a variety of sizes and shapes.

Eggplants used to be salted to reduce the bitterness in the flesh. This is not necessary with many modern varieties, although salting will help reduce the amount of oil the eggplant soaks up as it cooks. The fruit is fairly perishable and should ideally be stored at room temperature for up to a week or stored in the fridge for about two weeks. Once cut, the eggplant will darken and become bitter over time. Eggplant contains a range of vitamins and minerals and is a good source of dietary fibre. It is rich in phytonutrients, many of which have antioxidant qualities. An important phytonutrient is nasunin, a phenolic compound that is linked to maintaining brain health. Eggplant also contains modest levels of nicotine (more than most other vegetables).

The plant is a tropical perennial and needs help from black plastic mulch or a sunny wall to prosper in our region. Traviata is a dependable Italian dark oval type. Japanese varieties include Orient Express or Machiaw. Heirloom varieties include Barbarella (segmented purple), Kermit (mini green and white Thai eggplant), and Fairy Tale (mini variegated purple and white). For best fruiting, you really need a polytunnel, greenhouse, or a spot below a south facing wall for these heat-loving plants.

Okra (*Abelmoschus esculent sp.*)

Okra is a flowering plant (related to hibiscus) and we commonly eat the edible seedpods. The plant belongs to the mallow family, and is believed to have originated in Southeast Asia or Northern Africa. It is extremely low in calories and is a good source of vitamins A, C, K, and B complex as well as minerals like iron, calcium, and potassium. It also contains beta-carotene and lutein, which are beneficial to eye health. The plant contains a mucilaginous substance that is high in soluble fibre and helps with digestion. This characteristic means it is used to thicken stews like gumbo. The effect will be lessened if you cook the okra with an acidic ingredient like tomatoes or lemon juice.

Okra is a warm-region crop and needs to be planted later in the season when the soil has warmed up. After that, it matures quickly and will produce flowers and seedpods. Clemson Spineless is the only variety we have grown at the farm. It is an old heirloom variety and is hardy, a good producer, and easy to grow. Okra is not a good storing vegetable and is best eaten fresh or within a few days. Store okra in a paper bag in the fridge for best results.

Peppers (*Capsicum spp.*)

The pepper family, also known as capsicum in many parts of the world, consists of more than twenty-five species, five of which are commercially important. The plant originated in the Americas and has been transported worldwide. Sweet peppers (*C. annuum*) are mild and sometimes called bell peppers, or simply "peppers," modified by their color (green, red, yellow, orange, purple, etc.). Spicy peppers are usually referred to as chili peppers (or just chilies) and have many varieties. There is a bit of blurring in the categories, with peppers like Anaheim having the qualities of both.

The heat from spicy chilies comes from a component called capsaicin (*methyl vanillyl nonenamide*). This produces the heat and burning sensation we love. It is part of the fruit's natural defence mechanism to protect it from attack by insects. Capsaicin is heavily concentrated in the membrane surrounding the seeds. The amount of capsaicin varies greatly and the concentration is measured as Scoville heat units. Sweet peppers hover around 0 units, jalapeños vary from 2,000 to 10,000 units, and at the top of the scale are super-hot peppers like the Ghost pepper, at over 2 million units (now that's face-melting heat!).

Peppers are fairly perishable once picked. Traditionally the harvest was dried and/or smoked to preserve it for long periods. The fruit will last several weeks in the fridge before starting to break down. Peppers with a higher sugar content (like sweet peppers) are more perishable.

Peppers are a warm-region plant, and growing peppers in our region often produces mixed results. Many gardeners use green-houses, covered tunnels, and black plastic mulch to capture as much heat as possible. Many varieties are grown here: from the bell varieties (such as California Wonder and Orange Sun) to Mexican peppers (such as Adobe and Pasilla) to hot varieties (such as Jalapeño, Thai Dragon, and Scotch Bonnet).

Squash (*Cucurbita sp.*)

Squash originated in southern Mexico, Central America, and in regions of the Andes of South America. The plant has been an important source of food, medicine, and oil for many thousands of years. There are five domesticated species, most of which contain cultivars we call winter squash. One species (*C. pepo*) contains the species we call summer squash (zucchini and friends). Most species are vines, but several bush cultivars have been selectively developed. The plant produces male (pollen) and female (fruiting) flowers that rely on insects (mainly bees) to cross-pollinate.

The fruit is an excellent source of nutrients and is very high in vitamins A and C, as well as niacin, folic acid, beta-carotene, magnesium, and iron. The flesh is carbohydrate dense and contains beneficial starches and polysaccharides that contribute strong immune system-boosting qualities. It also contains a number of antioxidants and components like lutein and zeaxanthin, thought to contribute to eye health. The seeds are a good source of protein, food energy, and dietary fibres. The plant also contains low levels of a toxin called cucurbitin, which is responsible for the bitter taste of squash. It has been selectively bred to low levels, but sometimes squash cross-pollinate and the bitterness reappears in some fruit. High levels of cucurbitin will make the plant taste bitter and should be avoided as they may cause gastrointestinal upsets.

Squash are very easy to grow and are low maintenance (if you can keep the deer out!). They are a staple of many gardens in our region and have adapted well to our climate. My favorite varieties of winter squash are Kaboucha (sweet deep orange flesh), Butternut (smooth golden flesh), Red Kuri (firm golden flesh), and many varieties of Acorn and Hubbard squashes (heck—they're all good!). Summer squash standouts include zucchini like Raven or Anton (green), Goldy or Golden Egg (yellow), and round hybrid varieties like One Ball (yellow) or Eight Ball (green).

Sweet Corn (*Zea mays var. saccharata*)

Sweet corn is a modern cultivar of maize that has been developed over the years to focus on sweet and tender kernels. The plant is thought to have originated in southern Mexico and has been eaten for almost 9,000 years. The fruit of a plant is a fibrous ear that is covered in silk (actually the stigma) and the kernels lining the core are wrapped in a layer of husk leaves. Most sweet corn kernels are yellow, white, or mixed in color. The original maize was multicolored with many variations, including black, purple, green, and red kernels.

Most sweet varieties are sold as hybrid corn and have been selectively bred to produce more sugar (and less starch), than traditional varieties. Genetically modified (GMO) sweet corn is available in our stores and in commercially produced foods. GMO corn seeds are not presently offered by consumer garden seed companies. These corns are specifically bred to increase resistance to insects and to lessen the effects of herbicide and insecticide issues in the group. Organic varieties are GMO-free in Canada and the US.

Corn is a highly nutritious vegetable with many vitamins (it's rich in K and C) and is high in antioxidants. It is an excellent source of insoluble fibres, which is great for the digestive track, feeding natural beneficial bacteria in the intestines. The fibre also helps to space out the absorption of sugars into the blood, helping to moderate spikes in blood sugar levels.

Growing corn in a home garden in the Pacific Northwest can be a challenge; the plant is prone to a number of diseases and moulds associated with our cool night temperatures. Unfortunately, when we do get a good crop, the gardener has to be quicker than the local raccoon population. You also need a lot of real estate to grow a good crop of corn. Despite these challenges, at the farm, we still try for the joy of picking a ripe cob off the plant and eating it raw in the field. There may be no finer flavor in the garden. Good varieties for our climate include Peaches and Cream (white and yellow super sweet SH2) and Kandy Korn (yellow super sweet SH2).

Tomatoes (*Solanum lycopersicum*)

The tomato is the edible fruit in the nightshade family, related to eggplant and potatoes. The species is believed to have originated in the Andes and was first cultivated as a food in Mexico. The first tomatoes were small yellow varieties, and they have been selectively bred over centuries to get the more than 7,500 cultivars we see today. Now we see red, yellow, white, pink, green, and variegated tomatoes in the market, with more coming each year. The Spanish are credited with the spread of tomatoes to North America, Europe, and beyond. At first, Europeans thought the tomato was poisonous, and the leaves are in fact toxic. The fruit, however, is sweet and delicious and packed with nutrients and antioxidants. Lycopene has been associated with anticancer properties and helps to create strong bones. The fruit also contains many phytonutrients associated with heart health and building the immune system. Tomatoes are an outstanding source of vitamin C, B complex vitamins, and a range of other vitamins and minerals. It is classed near the top of the most nutritious foods list.

Fresh tomatoes from the garden are one of the joys of life. The sugars and cell structure start to break down when the fruit is harvested. Cold makes the cell structure rupture and results in a mealy texture. To compensate for this, many modern tomatoes are picked green and ripened with ethylene gas. Tomato varieties that put an emphasis on storage life, and even red colors, over taste and texture have been developed. Local greenhouse production has risen as a means of producing better varieties of eating tomatoes throughout the growing season.

Most tomato plants are classified as hybrid, open-pollinated, or heirloom. Hybrid is a plant that has been genetically crossed with two or more varieties for selected traits. If you plant the seeds from the plant, it may not duplicate the same characteristics. Open-pollinated and heirloom varieties are plants that produce seeds that will replicate the same characteristics. Open-pollinated signifies that pollination occurs by natural methods like birds, insects, and animals. The term heirloom refers to the human interaction of growing the plant and saving the seeds. All heirloom plants are open-pollinated and refer to those that were grown historically to produce consistent plants.

Tomatoes ripen best on the vine and should be left there as long as possible. When the fall evenings become cool, the flesh will blemish and blacken. That is your sign to pick all the tomatoes and continue to ripen them on a window sill, or use them to make a variety of green tomato dishes. Store them at cool room temperatures (ideally around 59°F/15°C) out of direct sunlight. Tomatoes need to be kept dry and benefit from being wrapped individually in paper (like old newspapers). They will keep longer if the stem is still attached to the fruit. Removing the stem leaves a scar that can allow bacteria to enter the tomato and accelerate the decay process. You do not need to retain the entire stem, just keep the leafy connection to the tomato top.

Tomatoes can be grown from seed or transplants. In cooler northern climates, they are often started in greenhouses and transplanted to the garden (or container) when the soil warms up. Tomatoes do not like cold nights or strong winds and should be sheltered from both. There are probably too many favorite types for me to list—at one point we had over fifty varieties going on the farm. If I had to go to a desert island, I would take a beefy tomato (like Brandywine), a paste tomato (like San Marzano), a cherry tomato (like Golden Sunburst), and a sweet green tomato (like Green Zebra).

INFLORESCENCE VEGETABLES
Some vegetables are actually clusters of flowers arranged on a stem. The flowers, flower buds, stems, and leaves are eaten as vegetables. These vegetables have great nutritional value and are often tender and very flavorful foods. Artichokes, broccoli, and cauliflower are common examples.

Artichokes (*Cynara cardunculus var. scolymus*)
The artichoke is a perennial plant native to the Mediterranean and is in the same species as the cardoon. We eat the small budding flower

head, peeling off the tough outer petals to reach the tender core (often called the artichoke heart). The artichoke is a warm-climate plant that usually takes two years to mature, but new cold-hearty cultivars that produce in the first year of growth are available. Other varieties must be overwintered before producing an abundant crop. If an artichoke survives the winter, it can produce for several years.

Artichokes are renowned as a delicacy and have many medicinal properties. The heart has some of the highest antioxidant levels reported for any vegetable. It also contains an interesting compound called cynarin, a chemical that inhibits taste receptors and alters the taste of some food and drink (notably wine, which is notoriously hard to pair with artichokes). Artichokes are known for aiding digestion and contain compounds that may improve the function of the liver and other organs. They contain excellent levels of vitamins K, C, and the B complex.

Choose artichokes that are firm and "squeak" when squeezed. Artichokes store well and will keep for a couple of weeks after harvest. During trimming, the exposed flesh of the heart will oxidize quickly and so is usually placed in a bath of water acidulated with lemon juice, vinegar, or vitamin C. Artichokes can be pickled or roasted and are excellent grilled.

Artichokes are fairly easy to grow. They require lots of sunlight, well-drained soil, and constant watering. Imperial Star is a fast-maturing plant bred to mature in the first year. Golden Globe is a classic variety that produces over several years of growth.

Broccoli (*Brassica oleracea*)

Broccoli is a member of the cabbage family; the large flowering head and stem are eaten. The plant is native to the Mediterranean and its name comes from the Italian *broccolo*, meaning "the flowering crest of cabbage." Broccoli is a developed cultivar of the *brassica* family. It is closely related to cauliflower, kale, and rapini.

Broccoli is high in vitamin C and dietary fibre. It also contains diindolylmethane, a compound with powerful antibacterial and anti-inflammatory properties. There are many other phytonutrients present, including carotenoids and lutein, that are reputed to have powerful anticancer and immune system-boosting properties. Boiling leaches some of these elements out during cooking. Steaming and sautéing are shown to retain much higher levels of these nutrients.

The most common type of broccoli is Calabrese broccoli, the green bunching head variety that is sold in all the markets.

A second type, called sprouting broccoli, is grown for smaller bunching heads of flowers. Romanesco broccoli (sometimes called Romanesco cauliflower) is a tightly packed flower head that has fantastic geometric shapes. It also comes in striking colors like lime green and purple.

Broccoli is a cool-weather crop that grows best in the cooler climates of the spring and fall. It tends to bolt when the temperatures climb in the mid to late summer. Broccoli should be harvested before the flower buds on the head have a chance to open and expand. The sprouting varieties are more heat tolerant and will produce well into the summer. Try head varieties like Calabrese and Centennial, sprouting types like Red Spear and Santee, and Romanesco types like Natalino and Minaret.

A subset of broccoli is broccoli rabe, or rapini. It looks similar to sprouting broccoli but has a slightly bitter taste. It grows and matures quickly. Varieties to try are Sorrento or Zamboni.

Cauliflower (*Brassica oleracea*)

Cauliflower is a brassica cultivar that was selectively bred to initially produce large white flower heads. New cultivars have been produced that feature yellow, orange, purple, and light green heads. The name comes from Latin and literally means cabbage flower. Like all the brassicas, the plant was native to the Mediterranean (possibly Cyprus) and was cultivated and manipulated in other parts of Europe. It is believed the first types were the Romanesco varieties, and the pure white varieties evolved from the ongoing selection of paler varieties until the white versions were produced.

Cauliflower is an excellent source of vitamins C and K and contains substantial quantities of minerals, dietary fibre, and phytonutrients. Many of these of these nutrients are thought to contain powerful anti-inflammatory properties and help the work of our purification organs like the liver and kidneys. Cauliflower is gentle on the digestive system and is even thought to ease the digestive process.

Cauliflower is a cool-weather crop, best timed for growing in the spring or fall. It is a little more high maintenance than its cousin broccoli and doesn't like extreme temperatures or prolonged stages of drought. Once you harvest the main head you can come back and harvest the smaller florets. The leaves should cover the white varieties to keep them creamy white. Choose white varieties like Shasta and Snow Crown, orange varieties like Sunset or Cheddar, purple varieties like Rosalind and the vivid Grafitti and green varieties like Monte Verdi and Panther.

LEAFY VEGETABLES

Once known as pot-herb, leafy vegetables are plant leaves that are the main edible part of the plant. The number of varieties approach 1,000 and most are sourced from cabbage, lettuce, and spinach. Most leafy vegetables have excellent nutritional value and high amounts of vitamins C and K. They also have a high moisture content, which makes many of the varieties fairly perishable.

Arugula (*Eruca sativa*)

Arugula (also called rocket) is a popular salad vegetable and cooking herb. It is a pungent leafy green vegetable and the stem, leaves, and flowers are edible. The plant is native to the Mediterranean, where it was originally harvested as a wild plant, and was then cultivated and spread to many parts of the planet.

The plant is well known for its strong, spicy flavor and is believed to have stimulant properties. In salads it is eaten alone or mixed with milder greens to mellow the flavor. Arugula is rich in vitamins, minerals, antioxidants, and phytonutrients. Its vitamins include excellent levels of vitamin K and good levels of vitamin C and the B complex. It contains significant amounts of a phytochemical group called indoles, powerful antibacterial and antiviral compounds that are also believed to benefit the respiratory system.

Arugula is easy to grow and can be harvested all year long, frequently overwintering in the garden. There are not many varieties available; most are just called conventional arugula or rocket. There is a relatively new cultivar called Speedy that matures slightly faster and is good as a second sowed varietal in the fall. Wild arugula (*Diplotaxis muralis* or *D. tenuifolia*) is a heartier and spicier form of arugula.

Brussels Sprouts (*Brassica oleracea*)

The Brussels sprout is a developed cultivar of the cabbage family. The sprouts even look like miniature cabbages. Brussels sprouts are frost hardy and even benefit from a little frost to develop flavor and sweetness. In mild years the plant can be harvested all winter long. Most varieties are green, but new purple and variegated cultivars are available.

Like many brassicas, Brussels sprouts contain excellent levels of vitamin C and K, plus B complex vitamins, folic acid, essential minerals, and dietary fibre. There is also an excellent array of phytonutrients like sulphoraphane and members of the indoles group.

Brussels sprouts are hardy plants that do well in our climate;

good green varieties are Nautis and Igor. Red varieties tend to produce a little less fruit but are beautiful on the plate—look for Red Ball.

Cabbage (*Brassica oleracea sp.*)
Cabbage is a leafy biennial plant that descended from the wild field cabbage and became the foundation for many of the vegetables we consume today. Varieties can be smooth skinned, crinkle leafed, green, purple, or white. Cabbage is composed of multiple layers of leaves and is very cold-tolerant. It is thought to be European in origin, but it quickly spread to many parts of the world once cultivated.

Cabbage is an excellent source of vitamins C, K, and B6 and folate. Its real powerhouse nutrients are antioxidants and phytonutrients with many antibacterial and immune system-boosting properties. Red and purple varieties contain anthocyanins, which are thought to provide anticancer properties in our diets.

There are three main types of cabbage varieties: white, red, and savoy. White includes the smooth-skinned green cabbages; most are round, but some have slightly pointy tops. Red cabbage includes purple and variegated varieties. Savoy cabbages are characterized by crinkled or curly leaves with a mild flavor and texture. They are all hardy in our area and relatively easy to grow.

Chinese cabbage (*Brassica rapa*, subspecies *pekinensis* and *chinensis*) can refer to two distinct varieties of Chinese leaf vegetables often used in Chinese cuisine. *Pekinensis* includes sui choy (or napa cabbage) and *chinensis* includes a complex family including bok choy. All these variants are descendants of the Western species. In Asia, the development was focused on different leaf forms.

In general, *pekinensis* cabbages have broad green leaves with white stems, tightly wrapped in a cylindrical formation and forming a loosely compact head. As the group name indicates, this is particularly popular in northern China around Beijing (Peking). *Chinensis* varieties don't form heads but have smooth green leaf blades like mustard. The most common subspecies is bok choy; Shanghai bok choy is a light green variant.

Chicory (*Cichorium spp.*)
Common chicory (*C. intybus*) includes radicchio and Belgian endive (also called Witloof Chicory). Curly endive (*C. endivia*) is a related species that includes frisée and escarole. Curly endive is fine leafed and finely textured; escarole is a broad-leafed version that is slightly less bitter. The naming of chicory and endive is very confusing as

there is lots of overlap between species, with many local names mixed in. For example, Belgian endive is not a true endive but is a member of the chicory family. All chicories have a mild to strong bitter taste and can be eaten raw, dressed in salads, sautéed, and cooked into soups and stews as a green.

Chicory is rich in many vitamins and minerals, especially in folate and vitamins A and K. It is also an excellent source of dietary fibre and is thought to aid in digestion. Phytonutrients include inulin (thought to help regulate blood sugars) and a number of carotenes, believed to strongly benefit the immune system.

Chicory cultivation depends on the variety, but most are easy to grow and harvest quickly. Some varieties are blanched to reduce bitterness and produce pale, cream-colored leaves (like frisée and Belgian endive).

Cress (*Lepidium sativum*)

Cress is also referred to as garden cress or pepper cress. The plant's origin is a little murky, with claims being made for Persia, North Africa, the eastern Mediterranean, and India. It is a fast-growing herb with many nutritional and medicinal properties, and is genetically related to mustards and watercress. It is also fairly perishable and should be used soon after harvest.

Cress is easy to grow and the edible shoots can be harvested in one to two weeks after planting. Look for the Cressida variety and a large smooth variant called Persian Cress.

Kale (*Brassica oleracea—Acephala Group*)

Kale is a vegetable that is considered to be closer to the original form of wild cabbage than many other domesticated forms now available. It is believed to have originated in the Mediterranean Basin. The cultivar group *Acephala* also includes spring greens and collard greens, which are genetically similar. Kale is a particularly robust plant that has spread and been naturalized as a wild plant in many parts of the world.

Kale is very high in beta carotene and vitamins K and C, and is rich in calcium. Kale is a good source of two carotenoids associated with eye health, lutein and zeaxanthin. It also contains sulphoraphane and indole compounds, chemicals linked to potent anticancer properties. These are water soluble and are diminished by boiling the vegetable. Sautéing and steaming are far better ways to preserve these nutrients. It is a fairly perishable plant and should be stored in the fridge and used within one week of harvest.

The three main types of commonly eaten kale include Curly Leaf (Scottish), which sports ruffled leaves and can be very tender and mild when fresh and young, becoming tougher and stronger flavored as it ages. Lacinto Kale is a hearty version with dark purple-green leaves and a ruffled surface texture (excellent for baking and retaining texture). Red Russian kale has delicate cut leaves with a red-purple stem. It is very tender and is often grown as a baby kale for salad mixes. All kales are easy to grow and low maintenance. Some varieties are self-seeding; curly leaf kale has been appearing on our farm (on its own) for the past fifty years. The previous owners were of Scottish descent, a family called the Smarts. We call it the "Smart Kale" in their honor.

Lettuce (*Lactuca sativa*)

Lettuce is an annual plant of the daisy (*Asteraceae*) family. Wild lettuce has a fairly big range, and the plant is thought to have originated in a wide swath through Europe to the Middle East. It was first domesticated by the Egyptians, who selectively bred the wild plant to produce succulent leaves. The name comes from the Latin *lactua* for the latex milk that exudes from the stem of the cut plant.

Lettuce is most often eaten raw in salads, but it also braised as a vegetable or used as a pot-herb in stews and soups and in Chinese dishes like fried rice. Lettuce is a good source of vitamins A and K, with higher concentrations of vitamin A found in darker green lettuces. Lettuce also provides potassium, some vitamin C, calcium, iron, and copper, with the vitamins and minerals being largely found in the leaf. Lettuce also naturally absorbs and concentrates lithium (implicated in improving mood and possibly beneficial for brain health). It provides some dietary fibre (concentrated in the spine and ribs), carbohydrates, protein, and a small amount of fat. Because of its fast-growing characteristics and use of copious water, lettuce has been implicated in contamination issues (like *E. coli*). The high water content of lettuce also creates problems when attempting to preserve the plant. It does not hold well and should be eaten fairly fresh. Once separated from the stem, the leaves should be washed and spun dry before short-term storage. Soaking also removes surface contamination and refreshes the structure of the lettuce.

Lettuce is usually grown quickly and tends to bolt and become very bitter if left to mature. This quick growth necessitates lots of nutrients and water. Other than that, it is relatively easy to cultivate. A number of pests (including deer!) love the plant for its tender, sweet leaves. Row covers of light fabric are a good idea in our region. Lettuce grows best in full sun in loose, nitrogen-rich soils.

There are seven main cultivars of lettuce (some are grown for oil from the seeds), but only five main types appear in our markets. We grow many varieties for diversity and harvesting throughout the year. The main types of Pacific Northwest cultivated lettuces are leaf lettuce (like Oak Leaf and Lolla Rosso), romaine (like Coastal Star and Valmine) iceberg/crisp (like Steamboat or Red Iceberg), butter (like Buttercrunch and Speckled Butterhead), and French crisp (like Cardinal and Nevada). Many other types work well either as whole head lettuce or plants grown for individual leaves or part of a great salad mix. We live in a great area for growing salad greens.

Spinach (*Spinacia oleracea*)

Spinach is an edible flowering plant in the family of *Amaranthaceae*. The plant originated in central and southwestern Asia, with some pinpointing the place of origin as Persia. When the plant reached China it was embraced, and many of the improvements in plant varieties occurred there—such as removing its bitterness and making the leaves more tender than the wild versions' leaves.

Spinach has a high nutritional value and can be eaten fresh, steamed, or quickly sautéed or blanched. It is a rich source of vitamins A, C, and K, as well as magnesium, manganese, folate, and iron. However, it also contains iron absorption-inhibiting oxalate, which can bind to the iron and render much of it unusable by the body. Cooking releases some of the oxalic acid and will improve the absorption rate. Spinach is similar to lettuce in its storage needs (short-term only) and should be washed and spun dry before use. It freezes well and is often steamed or wilted with heat (then chilled) before being frozen.

There are three main types of spinach. Flat or smooth-leafed spinach is the type we usually see in the stores. Try varieties like Olympia, Corvair, or Viroflay. Savoy spinach has dark crinkly leaves with a firmer texture and an intense green flavor. Try varieties like Bloomsdale or Samish. Semi-savoy is a hybrid variety that combines the best characteristics of the other two. Try varieties like Tyee or Vancouver.

GLOSSARY OF COOKING TERMS

Plants have some unique properties that distinguish them from meats or fungi. Many of the same techniques are used for cooking them, but they are often working on different physical and chemical attributes. For example, one of the key techniques in cooking is the browning of food. In meats this is largely caused by something called the Maillard reaction. This reaction is the interplay between amino acids and natural sugars found in meats, dairy products, and some vegetables. The result is a product that we think has a highly desirable flavor. Studies have shown that this flavor goes to the brain as pure pleasure. At higher temperatures, the sugar caramelizes and adds greatly to the pleasure factor. In essence, when we heat and brown food we are creating deep, complex caramel flavors and enhancing the pleasure factor in our brain. In vegetables, we often deal in a simpler caramelization of sugars, unless of course we add meat and dairy (like butter) to the mix. There is a smaller window of error with caramelization, as once sugar is heated to a certain level the process turns to carbonization—known to us all as burning (although a little charring, particularly on the grill, can be a good thing). Knowing the difference between the two is the key to turning good food into great food.

Chefs use tricks like these all the time, whether we are grilling, stir-frying, roasting, or braising our vegetables. Understanding the browning process is one key to making delicious, memorable food. Of course, that is not the way we eat all our vegetables; raw, steamed, blanched, and even microwaved vegetables are delicious and perhaps a little purer in flavor. They rely on the natural properties of the vegetables and usually a seasoning of some kind to make a big flavor statement.

The goal with your diet should be diversity and balance. The following terms explore a little of the background behind the cooking techniques in this book that help us achieve these goals.

BLANCHING

One of the fundamental techniques in a professional kitchen is blanching vegetables. This technique accomplishes several key functions. First, vegetables are blanched to partially cook them and then chilled in cold water. This prepares the food for quick cooking when meals are ordered. It also stops the decay process momentarily and keeps them in peak condition for several hours until they can be finished. It helps to break down cellulose in many vegetables, making them tender and sometimes creamy. Fennel is a good example of a vegetable that transforms from tough and fibrous to soft and deliciously creamy.

The key is to only cook the vegetables until they are just tender, similar to the concept of *al dente* in cooking pasta. You want to retain the crisp texture of the vegetable, but lessen the toughness of the vegetable fibres.

Usually the vegetables are blanched in salted, boiling water. The salt helps to season the vegetables and in the case of some it helps to set the color of chlorophyll and carotene—creating brighter green or orange colors. It also helps breaks down the cellular walls of the plant, making greens like spinach and kale or herbs like basil or arugula much easier to purée.

For best results, the vegetables are plunged in ice-cold water and drained as soon as the vegetable cools and chills slightly. At that point the vegetables can be placed in a container and stored under refrigeration for several hours until needed. One of the downsides of blanching is that many nutrients are water-soluble and tend to leach into the blanching liquid (which is salty and usually discarded).

STEAMING

Steaming, like blanching, is another method of cooking that does not rely on browning to develop more complex flavors. Usually sauces and flavoring are added once the food is cooked. Steaming works by placing the food over boiling water and enveloping it with hot vapors. Steaming has the advantage of cooking the food quickly with minimal loss of nutrients. The downside is that the equipment is a little more time-consuming to set up and clean. Steaming is also very efficient and the food must be carefully watched to ensure it does not overcook.

Another key advantage of steaming is that the food can be cooked in the absence of fat. It also helps to retain key nutrients like folic acid and vitamin C. Many phytonutrients (such as glucosinolates) and other antioxidants are better retained after a brief steaming. Steaming also helps release some of these nutrients, making them more readily available for digestion and assimilation into our bodies.

SAUTÉING / STIR-FRYING

Sautéing is a high-heat technique of cooking that usually involves a little oil to lubricate the process. The word comes from French and literally means to jump, referring to the tossing action of the food as it cooks. It is very similar to the Chinese technique of wokking. Both rely on high heat to sear the exterior, browning the sugars on the surface and allowing the interior to warm through. This is a technique where high heat is critical for flavor development; it relies on the Maillard reaction and caramelization to achieve deep flavor.

A little fat, in the form of oil, butter, or even animal fats like duck or pork, enhances these reactions.

The oil helps to slightly delay the process of scorching or burning the sugars and forming bitterness. It also helps to separate the vegetables and allow them to be tossed and tumbled for a more even heating action. You can stir the pan with a wooden spoon, but the best habit to develop is the technique of tossing the contents. Gently shake the pan and, with gentle flick of the wrist, roll the vegetables against the far side of the pan. This move looks dramatic in the professional kitchens, but is easy to master with a little practice. Practise with a cold skillet and a few dried beans and you will soon be ready to sauté with the best.

Other key points are to not overcrowd the pan to allow steam to escape, and to keep all the similar ingredients roughly the same size. You need to have everything chopped and ready to go before you start. In professional terms this is called *mise en place* (or "in its place"). You will have no time to chop much on the fly once the sautéing starts. Non-stick pans are great for sautéing; I use aluminum pans lined with a ceramic coating. Woks also work well, as do steel or cast iron pans (although they're heavier to toss). All these metal pans benefit from being well seasoned (cleaned, rubbed with oil, and heated). This builds up a thin layer of glaze that acts as a non-stick coating for the pan.

BRAISING

Braising is another great technique for developing flavor. Usually the vegetables are browned slightly to develop color and then cooked in a liquid (often flavored). The liquid forms a sauce and allows nutrients to be released and retained. These can be turned into sauces, soups, stews, and other dishes. The term comes from the Latin word for coals. Before ovens, dishes were placed directly on the fire to cook. Liquid helped to keep the dish from burning and created a delicious sauce at the end.

Braising relies on heat, time, and moisture to break down the fibres and nutrients in vegetables. The best braising equipment is a heavy ovenproof pan with a lid. It evenly distributes heat and does not allow hot spots to form and scorch the food. Cast iron coated with enamel is a great choice. You can also use a stainless steel roasting pan tightly covered with aluminum foil. The modern electric crock pot is another form of braising equipment.

ROASTING

Roasting is a key technique that can be used with many heat sources. Ovens, wood-burning ovens, and barbecues can all be used to roast foods. The process is usually dry, although a little oil and liquid might be used. Flavors are developed by heat penetrating the outside of the food and creating caramelization and Maillard browning. The air flow around the product has a big effect on the process and many modern ovens use fans to create convection and speed up the cooking. Wood ovens have great natural convection due to the intake of cool air and the exhaust of super-heated air up the chimney.

With vegetables, high heat is often better; you want the surface to caramelize and even slightly char in the case of some vegetables (like squash). The size of the cut is also important in roasting vegetables. You want even and consistent roasting. The larger the pieces, the more time it will take to cook them through. If you are cooking whole vegetables, like eggplant or a whole hollowed squash, you might want to use a lower and slower oven temperature to prevent the exterior from over charring before the interior has finished cooking. The best roasting pan is made from heavy gauge stainless steel or steel coated in enamel. These promote even heating and retain heat well—speeding up the process and helping foods caramelize evenly.

GRILLING

Grilling is another dry cooking method that relies on browning and caramelization to develop flavors. Many types of heat can be used, though today natural gas or propane are most often used. Wood, compressed wood pellets, lump charcoal, and compressed charcoal pellets (briquettes) are other choices. We tend to use all of these fuel sources on the farm for different effects. Wood imparts the most flavor; lump charcoal and briquettes add strong flavors and intense heat; gas is convenient and versatile—suitable for grilling, baking, and rotisserie cooking.

With vegetable grilling, a little oil is usually added to the outside, along with seasoning. This helps to evenly caramelize the sugars and adds greatly to the flavor of the finished product. This is another dry heat method that does not leach water-soluble nutrients. Slight charring is also desirable in grilling vegetables—it creates complex (sometimes bitter) flavors that balance out the natural sweetness.

SMOKING

Smoking is the process of flavoring, cooking, or preserving (drying) food by exposing it to smoke from burning or smouldering material. Most often this is from wood, but tea, sugar, spices, and herbs can also be added. Traditionally, many farms in our region had smoke houses for smoking meats and seafood such as salmon. Modern technology has given us many forms of smoking equipment. Small metal box smokers are inexpensive and easy to operate. We often use a pellet smoker here on the farm. This is a technology that was developed for heating stoves and has been translated to barbecues and smokers. Compressed pellets of many types or blends of wood are used to create highly controllable amounts of smoke and heat.

Locally, alder is the traditional smoking wood, but oak is more often used as a base and to blend with other types of wood. Oak produces a clean and evenly finished product. Other woods are more aromatic and are often blended in for flavor. Apple, cherry, hickory, mesquite, and pecan are all used for different flavor profiles.

Cold smoking uses low-temperature smoke that dries the surface but does not substantially cook the product. Hot smoking uses a variety of higher temperatures to dry out and preserve the product while adding smoke, char, and caramelized flavors to the mix.

FERMENTING

Fermentation is a natural process that involves the action of microorganisms. It occurs from the conversion of carbohydrates to alcohols and carbon. Fermentation of food products is the use of controlled processes to create delicious, healthy foods. It creates lactic acid in foods like sauerkraut, kimchi, and yogurt. Fermentation is involved in the process to create vinegar (acetic acid), yeast-based goods, and of course, alcoholic beverages.

The process has many benefits, as both a preservative and a means of enriching food with available proteins, essential amino acids, and vitamins. It also enhances the flavor aroma and texture of foods. Controlling the process is critical—time, temperature, and wild organisms all play a role in the fermentation process. Cleaning all equipment and keeping out wild yeasts is important for obtaining consistent results with your fermenting. The Koreans add plenty of chilies as a natural antibacterial agent.

PREPARATION ESSENTIALS

A key part of cooking is preparing the ingredients before you actually begin to cook. How the ingredients are cut can affect their textural qualities, how evenly they cook, and whether the maximum nutrition is extracted from them. Some foods are so dense and fibrous that they must be shredded or thinly sliced before they are enjoyable to eat. Others benefit from being mashed or puréed before being consumed.

The most important piece of equipment you can have on hand is a good, sharp knife. Keeping a knife sharp is one of the first things we teach apprentices and students. A sharp knife makes the work go faster, reduces waste, and creates a firmer chopping action, allowing you to cut smoothly and safely. A dull knife occasionally deflects from the surface you are cutting, which can put you at risk of cutting yourself. This is particularly likely when you are cutting firm vegetables like squash and beets. With large squash, I like to use a large, firm serrated knife. This kind of blade bites into the firm flesh and easily saws through it.

You can improve your knife skills with practice. You'll have to put in a little time to gain confidence and work up to faster speeds, but in the home kitchen, speed is a relative concept (with no chef standing yelling over your shoulder). You would be better spending your time on striving to be efficient and learning to execute a variety of vegetable cuts to create interesting and nutritious food.

PEELING

The first question you should ask is: Do I really need to peel? Many nutrients sit just under the skin of many vegetables. If the skin is thin, it can usually be scrubbed and washed clean. Sometimes the skin is thick, blemished, or extremely dirty and gnarly (like the surface of celeriac). If you do have to peel—squash, for example, needs to be peeled to get down to the edible flesh—use a sharp peeler that takes off a thin layer of skin. Really tough skins can be cut off by using a serrated knife in a sawing motion.

SLICING

It is important to make the item you are cutting stable. Round vegetables like carrots tend to want to roll when you press a knife into them; one solution is to take a thin slice off their side. When you place the vegetable cut side down, it will be relatively stable and you can continue slicing. How thickly you slice affects the texture of foods that are eaten raw and affects the cooking time for cooked foods. And you won't always want to slice all your ingredients to the same thickness. For example, when you are cooking foods together in a stir-fry, you need to cut the dense foods (like carrots) thinner so they cook at the same speed as softer foods (like mushrooms). Every recipe in this book specifies a cut. For very thin slices (and for uniform results), chefs use a device called a mandolin. There are relatively inexpensive Japanese versions that the home cook can use to create several thin cuts of vegetables. But be careful: the blades are very sharp and unforgiving.

JULIENNING

The julienne is an important technique in the modern kitchen. In essence, it is a slice of vegetable cut into thin strips. For the most dramatic effect, the slices are taken off the longest edge of the vegetable to create long square shreds of vegetable. This is a technique you see a lot of in French, Thai, and Vietnamese food. It takes practice and is a good way to develop your knife skills. You can also use a mandolin to shred the vegetable into a thin and consistently even strip.

DICING

To dice, you cut the vegetable into a thick slice and then cut the slice into thick strips. The strip is then cut into pieces to make roughly square pieces. The thickness of the initial slice governs the thickness of the final dice. For most finished dishes, a fine dice of around ¼ inch (roughly ¾ cm) is used. This is what you would need to make a salsa or for adding diced mushrooms to a sauce. A medium dice is around ½ inch (1.25 cm) and is a good size for soups and chowder. A large dice (sometimes referred to as a cube) is about 1 inch (2.5 cm), and is a nice size for stews and roasting vegetables.

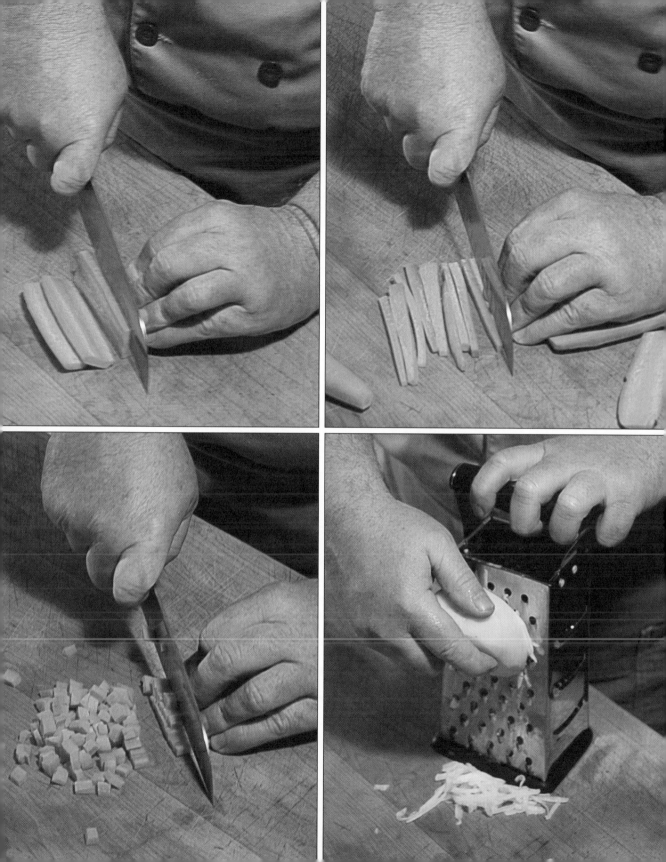

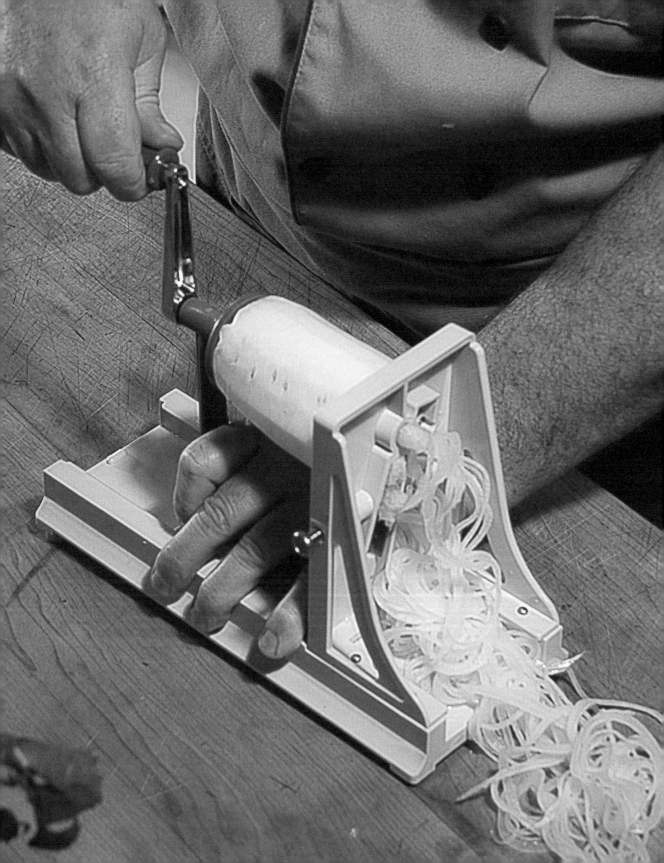

SHREDDING

Dense or fibrous vegetables like cabbage or carrots are often shredded to make them easier to chew or to create an interesting texture. Leafy vegetables (like cabbage) are often shredded with a large chef's knife. You can also use a box grater, the shredding disc on a food processor, or a number of gadgets to create a fine shred. One gadget we use in the kitchen is a Japanese vegetable shredder that produces a continuous shred. This device spins the vegetable (daikon radish, carrot, and beet all work well) to create a long, thin, continuous shred. These make excellent visual additions to salads and can be used to create a kind of vegetable "pasta."

PAIRING WINE WITH VEGETABLE DISHES

We are lucky to live in a region with lots of excellent local wine. It makes sense to pair local food with local wine. They both spring from the same earth and share the qualities of place that the French call *terroir*. When used in moderation, wine aids digestion and has some relaxation and stress-relief properties. Pairing wine with vegetable recipes is a similar process to pairing it with any other dish. Sometimes you want the wine to complement the dish, other times a nice contrast works well and brings balance to your meal. There are many reasons the pairing can work magic, with the most obvious being that you like the taste of both.

In general, vegetables dishes are modified by the cooking method, the level of sweetness and bitterness, and the fat content. In a pinch, almost anything you have on hand will work. The acidity, tannins, and sugars in wine tend to sweep the palate clean each time you swill it back. There are occasions when you want to make the food and wine work hand-in-hand, perhaps you have special guests or a nice wine you want to showcase. This is when the following tips for pairing wine will come in handy.

1. The cooking technique you use will affect the flavor of the vegetables. For example, steamed and roasted carrots present two different flavor profiles. If the dish has a strong and powerful flavor, it will cope with strong and powerful wines.
2. Don't be afraid to use some fat. Butter, olive oil, and cheese all positively modify the flavors of wine on your palate.
3. Pay attention to acidity. Vinegar or citrus in a dish will influence the wine match. Use a dry, acidic white wine or a light red wine to blend with these flavors.
4. Spices (like chili peppers) tend to dominate your palate and alter the taste of wine. This also works for smoky and salty flavors. Locally, this calls for a lighter red (like Pinot Noir or Cabernet

Franc) or even wines with a bit of sweetness, like off-dry (slightly sweet) Riesling, Gewürztraminer, or Viognier.

5. Some vegetables are like problem children—they just misbehave. Artichoke is a good example. It contains a compound called cynarin that acts to make most wines taste slightly bitter and metallic. Asparagus is another challenging match. Both of these work best with a dry, bright white wine. Pinot Blanc is a stellar local choice.

6. Some vegetables—caramelized onion, cooked garlic, and root vegetables, for example—make anything taste better. They introduce sweetness and caramel flavors that complement many wines.

One of the keys to matching wine successfully with vegetables is to look at the cooking method, and in particular the development of flavors through Maillard reactions and caramelization. Browning from these reactions creates sweet, bitter, and complex flavors that add to the intensity of the dish. Grilling, roasting, and sautéing build up these flavors and allow the dish to handle a more intense wine—like an oak barrel-aged Chardonnay or a big fruity red like a Shiraz or a Merlot.

A second key is to carefully choose the seasoning for the vegetable. Olive oil, butter (and all dairy), garlic, onion, and spices all boost the flavor profile and allow you to bring more intense wine flavor without overpowering the balance of the wine match. On the flip side, a nice bright wine tends to bring contrast and clean the palate between sips.

In general, vegetable dishes are on the lighter end of the scale and work best with the lighter- and medium-bodied wines. For most vegetable dishes, with a combination of ingredients, go for a regional white such as Pinot Gris, Pinot Blanc, Gewürztraminer, Chenin Blanc, Sauvignon Blanc, Riesling, or the Riesling cousins like Müller-Thurgau or Kerner. Lighter reds include the rosé (an all-round excellent match with many vegetable flavors), Cabernet Franc, Pinot Noir, Merlot, and lighter Syrah (also known as Shiraz). Another option is a sparkling wine, both white and red varieties.

Grilled dishes, or those made with cream or cheese, can handle the bigger wines. They match well with white wines that have been aged in oak, such as Chardonnay or Pinot Blanc, and with the lighter reds listed above. If the dish is heavy in dairy and strong flavors (like lasagna or a gratin), then an even bigger red wine such as Cabernet Sauvignon, fruity Zinfandel, a full-bodied Malbec, a big Syrah, or a bold house blend (like Meritage or Bordeaux blends) will work.

A number of vegetables work a special magic with wine pairings. Beans, corn, squash, and tomatoes are top of my list, and mushrooms, onions, garlic, and herbs also help to create a harmonious mix with wine.

NOTES ON USING THIS BOOK

ON INGREDIENTS

Apples: use any type, unless otherwise specified, though Fuji and Gala are recommended.

Butter: is salted and can be at room temperature, unless otherwise specified. You can substitute the same volume of coconut oil.

Cream: always use whipping cream. You can substitute the same volume of coconut milk.

Eggs: use large, as fresh as possible.

English cucumber (also known as Burpless): keep the skin on and use the seeds. You can also use Persian.

Frying oil: grapeseed is recommended, and rice bran and avocado are also good choices.

Maple syrup: use any grade. Medium and dark are best for baking.

Milk: use 2% or whole milk, unless otherwise specified. You can substitute the same volume of rice, almond, or coconut milk.

Mustard: use any type, whole grain, Dijon, or even yellow prepared mustard.

Olive oil: always use extra virgin.

Olives: always buy olives with their pits intact (any variety) and remove the pit just before use. Kalamata and green picholine are two of my favorites.

Pepper: use finely ground black pepper—fresh, if possible.

Potatoes: use any type, unless otherwise specified. Russet is best for mashed.

Salt: always use fine sea salt, unless otherwise specified.

Stock: when adding stock, it can be hot or cold, unless otherwise specified.

Sugar: use granulated unless otherwise specified.

Tomatoes: use any type, unless otherwise specified, and use the seeds. Paste tomatoes are best for sauces. If you want to remove the skin you can blanch the tomato for two to three minutes, chill it in cold water, and then remove the skin. For smooth sauces, you can cook the whole tomato, skin and all, then purée and strain through a sieve to remove both the skin and seeds.

ON KITCHEN EQUIPMENT

Casserole dishes: The best casserole dishes are cast iron with a ceramic coating. This will allow even heating and produce excellent crusts on the bottom and sides of the product. Glass and coated clay dishes also work well. The most common size is 13 × 9 inches (33 × 23 cm).

Lids: I seldom use lids when I'm cooking, even for things like soup. I do use a lid when cooking rice or grains like barley or couscous on the stovetop, though. In this book, everything cooked on the stovetop is cooked uncovered, unless otherwise specified.

Ovens: Every oven performs a little differently. I usually use the convection setting on my oven for most of the cooking. Convection uses a fan to circulate the air inside the oven. This produces faster browning (10–15 percent faster) and has the effect of increasing the temperature by about 25°F (14°C). The best advice is to keep an eye on a dish the first time you cook it and adjust the timing based on how your oven is performing.

Pans: Non-stick pans are used for most of the cooking. Look for pans that have been coated in ceramic (over a base of cast iron or aluminum) for the most environmentally friendly products. Uncoated steel or cast iron also work very well for frying and baking, although you should avoid adding acid (like tomato or citrus) to the pan, as this will leach a metallic taste into the dish.

Pots: Most of the pots I use are stainless steel, for the even heat distribution and ease of care. I do not recommend aluminum pots for the kitchen unless they are covered with a non-reactive coating like ceramic. A heavy-bottomed pot is critical for distributing heat and easing scorching. Good pots are an investment that will last a lifetime.

RECIPES

PANTRY
AND
PRESERVES

SAUERKRAUT AND VARIATIONS

Most sauerkraut recipes make enough to last you a winter. I prefer to make the kraut in small batches using a one-gallon glass Mason jar. This tends to last me for a couple of months. Feel free to make larger batches using the same ratio of ingredients.

MAKES ABOUT 12 CUPS (4 L)

....

2 heads green cabbage, about 5–6 lb
    (2.5–3 kg)
3 Tbsp (45 mL) salt

Cleanliness is crucial with fermented foods. Make sure the kitchen is clean and that all utensils, cutting boards, and jars are freshly washed in hot water. Air-dry just before using. I recommend cleaning the kitchen surfaces with vinegar to create a nice environment for clean fermentation. Just before chopping, wash all of the ingredients. Make sure to wash your hands as well.

Prepare the cabbage by removing any damaged or wilted outer leaves to get down to the crisp, waxy leaves. First cut each cabbage in half, and then quarter them. Remove the solid core of the cabbage. Shred the cabbage thinly with a sharp knife, place it in a bowl, and sprinkle the salt on top. Toss with a pair of kitchen tongs until well mixed. At this point you can add one or a combination of the ingredients listed on the facing page. Start with the traditional flavor of caraway and then experiment with other single or combined flavors. The possibilities are endless.

Mix the cabbage and flavoring (if using) and massage the cabbage and salt with your hands. Let it sit for 30 minutes, or until liquid begins to ooze out of the cabbage. Toss well to mix and place by the handful into the jar (or multiple jars, depending on the size of the cabbage). Pour the juice overtop of the cabbage. Fill each jar, leaving about one-quarter of the jar free at the top.

Place a weight (I use ceramic discs or small saucers) on top of the cabbage. Push down until the liquid covers the cabbage. Repeat this occasionally over the next 24 hours, keeping the jar on a countertop and covered with a clean kitchen cloth (hold it in place with a large rubber band if you like). If after 24 hours the liquid has not covered the cabbage (it depends on how fresh the cabbage is), you can dissolve 1 teaspoon (5 mL) of salt in 1 cup (250 mL) of water to make a brine to top up the sauerkraut. Place in a cool dark place (closet or pantry) and ferment for 7 to 10 days. Occasionally remove any scum or mould (harmless) that appears on top and add more brine if the liquid evaporates and the veg becomes exposed. Taste after 3 to 5 days and stop fermenting when the flavor is appealing to you (it will get stronger as it sits and ferments). Once ready, sauerkraut can be placed in a sealed glass jar and stored in the fridge for several months.

FLAVORINGS:
- 2 Tbsp (30 mL) whole caraway seeds
- 2 Tbsp (30 mL) grated ginger
- 2 apples, peeled and grated
- 1 large carrot, peeled and shredded
- 2 Tbsp (30 mL) whole fennel or mustard seeds
- 1 Tbsp (15 mL) dried chili flakes
- 2 Tbsp (30 mL) chopped fir needles, or rosemary or sage leaves

SPICY PICKLED BEETS WITH GINGER AND CINNAMON

I normally use baby red beets for this pickle. You can cut the beets into halves, quarters, or slices. I usually cook the beet with the skin on; this lessens the mess and minimizes the red staining. You will love the combination of beets, ginger, and cinnamon. The sweet earthy flavor of the beets really shines through.

MAKES ABOUT SIX (2-CUP [500 ML]) JARS

4 lb (about 1.6 kg) small beets, washed and trimmed
2 cups (500 mL) cider vinegar
1 cup (250 mL) demerara sugar
¼ cup (65 mL) ginger, very thinly sliced (about a 2-inch/5 cm piece)
1 stick cinnamon
1 Tbsp (15 mL) black peppercorns
1 small jalapeño pepper, quartered

Place the cleaned beets in a stockpot and cover with water. Bring to a boil, turn down the heat, and simmer for 20 minutes, or until the beets can be pierced easily with a small knife or skewer. Drain and allow to cool to room temperature. When cool enough to handle, use a small knife to remove the skin, scraping gently to loosen it. Remove the tops if desired. Reserve until needed.

Heat a heavy-bottomed saucepan over medium-high heat. Add 1 cup (250 mL) water with the cider vinegar, sugar, ginger, cinnamon, peppercorns, and jalapeño. For a little heat, add the chili pepper seeds (trim and discard the seeds and membrane for a milder flavor). Bring to a boil. Cut the beets into wedges (or slices depending on the size) and add to the pickling broth. Bring back to a boil and cook for 1 minute.

Meanwhile, wash your glass jars and rinse them in hot water. Place them on a rack to dry. When the beet mixture has been brought to a boil, remove it from the heat. Ladle the hot beets into six 2-cup (500 mL) jars. Top up with the hot liquid to within ¼ inch (0.6 cm) of the top of the jar. Tap the jar to remove any air bubbles and wipe the rim to remove any residue. Place a lid on top and screw the band down until resistance is met, then gently tighten. You can cool to room temperature and then store in the fridge, or heat process to create a more stable product (see page 79 for details). For best quality, use the beets within 1 year.

SHREDDED CARROTS WITH FIR NEEDLES

Grand fir is my favorite, but Douglas fir (widely available) and hemlock fir make a nice mix. Try to get the largest carrot possible for this dish—it will make the shredding a lot easier. The result is a combination of tart citrus flavor perfumed with the scent of Christmas.

MAKES ABOUT SIX (2-CUP [500 ML]) JARS

4 lb (about 1.6 kg) large carrots, peeled and trimmed

2 cups (500 mL) white vinegar

1½ cups (375 mL) sugar

¼ cup (65 mL) fir needles, stalks removed (grand fir, Douglas fir, or hemlock fir)

4 cloves garlic, peeled and sliced

Place a hand grater on a clean cutting board and shred the carrot coarsely. Meanwhile, wash your glass jars, rinse them in hot water, and place them on a rack to dry.

Heat a heavy-bottomed saucepan over medium-high heat. Add 1 cup (250 mL) water with the vinegar, sugar, fir needles, and garlic. Bring to a boil. Add the shredded carrot to the pickling broth. Bring back to a boil and cook for 1 minute.

Ladle the hot carrots into six 2-cup (500 mL) jars. Top up with the hot liquid to within ¼ inch (0.6 cm) of the top of the jar. Tap the jar to remove any air bubbles and wipe the rim to remove any residue. Place a lid on top and screw the band down until resistance is met, then gently tighten. You can cool to room temperature and then store in the fridge, or heat process to create a more stable product (see page 79 for details). For best quality, use the carrots within 1 year.

CUCUMBER WITH FENNEL SEEDS AND CHILIES

Use large field cucumbers for this recipe. They have more flavor and texture than the thin English or Persian cucumber. You can peel the cucumber, or leave it intact if you don't mind a little fibre in the mix. Use fresh fennel seeds if possible. If you only have dried seeds, gently toast them in a dry skillet to reactivate the essential oils.

MAKES ABOUT SIX (2-CUP [500 ML]) JARS

6 large field cucumbers

1 Tbsp (15 mL) salt

1 cup (250 mL) pickling vinegar

1 cup (250 mL) sugar

1 Tbsp (15 mL) fennel seeds

2 small jalapeño peppers, minced

2 Thai red chilies, chopped

Place a cucumber on a clean cutting board, peel if desired, and cut in half lengthwise. Using a spoon, scrape out and discard the seeds. Cut the halves into triangular wedges. Repeat with the remaining cucumber. Place the wedges in a bowl and sprinkle with the salt. Let sit as you prepare the pickling solution.

Heat a heavy-bottomed saucepan over medium-high heat. Add 1 cup (250 mL) water with the vinegar, sugar, fennel seeds, and jalapeño and Thai chilies. Bring to a boil. Drain the cucumber and add it to the saucepan. Bring to a boil and cook for 1 minute.

Meanwhile, wash your glass jars and rinse them in hot water. Place them on a rack to dry. Ladle the hot cucumbers into six 2-cup (500 mL) jars. Top up with the hot liquid to within ¼ inch (0.6 cm) of the top of the jar. Tap the jar to remove any air bubbles and wipe the rim to remove any residue. Place a lid on top and screw the band down until resistance is met, then gently tighten. You can cool to room temperature and then store in the fridge, or heat process to create a more stable product (see page 79 for details). For best quality, use the cucumbers within 1 year.

MIXED VEGETABLES, OLIVES, AND MUSTARD PICKLE

You can make this pickle with an assortment of vegetables like asparagus, green beans, and sweet peppers. Or try a mix of Asian vegetables like bok choy and gai lan. Taste the mix once it has cooked and add sugar, vinegar, and mustard to taste.

MAKES ABOUT SIX (2-CUP [500 ML]) JARS

2 large field cucumbers

1 tsp (5 mL) salt

2 cups (500 mL) pickling vinegar

1 cup (250 mL) sugar

½ cup (125 mL) whole grain mustard

2 Tbsp (30 mL) pickling spice

2 cups (500 mL) Kalamata olives

4 large carrots, trimmed and
   sliced thickly

1 head cauliflower, trimmed into
   small florets

Place a cucumber on a clean cutting board, peel if desired, and cut in half lengthwise. Using a spoon, scrape out and discard the seeds. Cut the halves into triangular wedges. Repeat with the remaining cucumber. Place the wedges in a bowl and sprinkle with the salt. Let sit as you prepare the pickling solution.

Heat a heavy-bottomed saucepan over medium-high heat. Add 1 cup (250 mL) water with the vinegar, sugar, mustard, pickling spice, olives, carrots, and cauliflower. Bring to a boil, turn down the heat to a simmer, and cook for 4 to 5 minutes, or until the vegetables are just tender. Drain the cucumber and add it to the saucepan. Bring back to a boil and cook for 1 minute.

Meanwhile, wash your glass jars and rinse them in hot water. Place them on a rack to dry. Ladle the hot cucumbers into six 2-cup (500 mL) jars. Top up with the hot liquid to within ¼ inch (0.6 cm) of the top of the jar. Tap the jar to remove any air bubbles and wipe the rim to remove any residue. Place a lid on top and screw the band down until resistance is met, then gently tighten. You can cool to room temperature and then store in the fridge, or heat process to create a more stable product (see page 79 for details). For best quality, use the pickle mix within 1 year.

QUICK PICKLED ONION WITH CARAMEL AND VIETNAMESE FLAVORS

Caramel is a big part of Vietnamese cooking and creates a harmony with the onions. You can also add a little fish sauce and fresh chilies to taste. This is a quick pickle that must be kept in the fridge and used within about a month.

MAKES ABOUT 10 CUPS (ABOUT 2.5 L)

2 lb (about 1 kg) red onions, peeled
   and thinly sliced

1 Tbsp (15 mL) salt

1 cup (250 mL) sugar

2 cups (500 mL) malt vinegar

1 Tbsp (15 mL) minced ginger

1 Tbsp (15 mL) minced garlic

1 Tbsp (15 mL) hot sauce

3 Tbsp (45 mL) chopped
   cilantro leaves

2 Tbsp (30 mL) chopped mint leaves

In a mixing bowl, place the red onion and sprinkle it with the salt. Let sit for at least 10 minutes while you make the pickling liquid.

Heat a heavy-bottomed saucepan over medium-high heat. Add 1 cup (250 mL) water with the sugar. Stir with a wooden spoon to dissolve. Cook until the sugar begins to caramelize, about 5 minutes. As the sugar begins to brown on the edges of the pot, swirl to distribute the caramel. Add the vinegar carefully—the sugar will create a lot of steam. Stir with a wooden spoon to dissolve the caramel. Add the onion slices and the ginger, garlic, and hot sauce, then the cilantro and mint. Bring to a boil and cook for 1 minute.

Meanwhile, wash a one-gallon glass jar and rinse it in hot water. Place it on a rack to dry.

Remove the saucepan from the heat and allow to cool. Transfer the contents to the glass jar, or a suitable airtight container. When cool, place in the fridge and chill for at least 4 hours, preferably overnight.

This will keep for up to 1 month refrigerated.

MAPLE AND GREEN TOMATO CHOW CHOW

I use a commercial pickling spice for this pickle with great results. I heat the spice mix in a dry skillet until aromatic (and not burning). After cooling, grind the mixture in a coffee or spice grinder until smooth. We use this as an accompaniment to eggs (any style) for breakfast, or as a general condiment for the table. Use a lower grade maple syrup (medium or dark) for best results.

MAKES ABOUT SIX (2-CUP [500 ML]) JARS

6 lb (about 2.5 kg) green tomatoes, cored and sliced

2 lb (about 1 kg) yellow onions, peeled and thinly sliced

¼ cup (65 mL) coarse sea salt

2 cups (500 mL) pickling vinegar

2 cups (500 mL) medium or dark maple syrup (or half maple syrup and half brown sugar)

¼ cup (65 mL) ground pickling spice

1 Tbsp (15 mL) minced ginger

1 Tbsp (15 mL) ground turmeric

In a large mixing bowl, place the tomatoes and onions. Sprinkle with the salt and toss to mix well. Cover with plastic film and let sit overnight. The next day, strain into a colander and gently press to remove any excess moisture.

Heat a heavy-bottomed saucepan over medium-high heat. Add the vinegar, maple syrup, pickling spice, ginger, and turmeric. Bring to a boil and add the tomato and onion mixture. Bring back to a boil, turn down the heat to a simmer, and cook for about 1 hour, stirring occasionally.

Meanwhile, wash your glass jars and rinse them in hot water. Place them on a rack to dry. Ladle the hot pickle mix into six 2-cup (500 mL) jars. Top up with the hot liquid to within ¼ inch (0.6 cm) of the top of the jar. Tap the jar to remove any air bubbles and wipe the rim to remove any residue. Place a lid on top and screw the band down until resistance is met, then gently tighten. You can cool to room temperature and then store in the fridge, or heat process to create a more stable product (see page 79 for details). For best quality, use the chow chow within 1 year.

PICKLED FENNEL WITH LEMON AND HONEY

Cooking fennel gives the flesh a soft and luscious texture. It is wonderful as an accompaniment to goat cheese or fresh hummus. If you like more crunch to the pickle, reduce the cooking time to about 1 minute. This will leave a little bite and texture.

MAKES ABOUT SIX (2-CUP [500 ML]) JARS

6 large fennel bulbs

1 Tbsp (15 mL) salt

1 cup (250 mL) honey

2 cups (500 mL) pickling vinegar

6 whole clove buttons

1 Tbsp (15 mL) whole black
    peppercorns

2 lemons, juice and zest

Remove any discolored outer leaves from the fennel and chop off any green tops. Wash the fennel and place it on a clean cutting board. Cut it in half and remove any solid core from the bulb. Using a sharp knife or mandolin, cut the fennel into very thin slices. Place them in a bowl and sprinkle with the salt. Let the fennel sit as you prepare the pickling solution.

Heat a heavy-bottomed saucepan over medium-high heat. Add 1 cup (250 mL) water with the honey, vinegar, cloves, peppercorns and the lemon juice and zest. Bring to a boil and then turn down the heat to a simmer. Cook the mixture for 5 minutes, or until the fennel softens slightly but still retains a bit of crispness.

Meanwhile, wash your glass jars and rinse them in hot water. Place them on a rack to dry. Ladle the hot fennel into six 2-cup (500 mL) jars. Top up with the hot liquid to within ¼ inch (0.6 cm) of the top of the jar. Tap the jar to remove any air bubbles and wipe the rim to remove any residue. Place a lid on top and screw the band down until resistance is met, then gently tighten. You can cool to room temperature and then store in the fridge, or heat process to create a more stable product (see page 79 for details). For best quality, use the fennel within 1 year.

FIVE-SPICE TOMATO JAM

You can make this jam with fresh, frozen, or canned tomatoes. If you use canned tomatoes, make sure you look for a low-salt version, or check the salt in the dish before adding any.

MAKES ABOUT SIX (2-CUP [500 ML]) JARS

8 lb (about 3.6 kg) ripe red tomatoes, cored and coarsely chopped

1 lb (454 g) yellow onions, peeled and diced

2 cups (500 mL) shredded carrot

1 cup (250 mL) diced celery

1 Tbsp (15 mL) minced ginger

1 Tbsp (15 mL) salt

1 cup (250 mL) honey

2 Tbsp (30 mL) white wine vinegar

2 Tbsp (30 mL) Five-Spice Powder (page 81)

1 tsp (5 mL) freshly ground nutmeg

Heat a heavy-bottomed saucepan over medium-high heat. Add the tomatoes, onions, carrot, celery, ginger, and salt. Stir until the liquid releases from the tomato and then turn down the heat to a simmer. Simmer the mixture for 10 to 15 minutes, or until all the vegetables are tender. Purée the mixture with an immersion blender, then strain it through a fine metal sieve. Use a spoon or ladle to push the liquid through the sieve, leaving behind the vegetable matter.

Return the liquid to the heavy-bottomed saucepan and add the honey, vinegar, Five-Spice Powder, and nutmeg. Simmer over low heat, stirring often, until the mixture thickens and coats the back of a spoon. Taste and adjust the seasoning with five-spice mixture, salt, and vinegar until a nice balance of sweet and sour is reached (it depends on how ripe the tomatoes are).

Meanwhile, wash your glass jars and rinse them in hot water. Place them on a rack to dry. Ladle the tomato jam into six 2-cup (500 mL) jars. Top up with the hot liquid to within ¼ inch (0.6 cm) of the top of the jar. Tap the jar to remove any air bubbles and wipe the rim to remove any residue. Place a lid on top and screw the band down until resistance is met, then gently tighten. You can cool to room temperature and then store in the fridge, or heat process (see facing page) to create a more stable product. For best quality, use the tomato jam within 1 year.

HEAT PROCESSING PRESERVES

Place filled jars in the rack of a canning pot. When canner is filled, make sure the jars are covered by at least 1 inch (2.5 cm) of water. Cover canner and bring water to full rolling boil, process for a full 10 minutes.

Turn stove off, remove canner lid, wait 5 minutes, then remove jars without tilting and place them upright on a cooling rack. Cool upright, undisturbed for at least a day.

Check each jar for a good seal. Sealed discs curve downward and do not move when pressed. Remove screw bands; wipe and dry bands and jars. Store screw bands separately or replace loosely on jars, as desired. Label and store jars in a cool, dark place. For best quality, use the beets within 1 year. Any jars that have not sealed should be stored in the fridge and used first.

FIVE-SPICE POWDER

Freshly made Five-Spice Powder is miles away from the storebought versions. You can double the recipe if you like. I tend to keep the raw materials on hand and can whip up a batch in a matter of minutes. This is one mixture that tastes much better with a freshly toasted and ground blend.

MAKES 5 TBSP (75 ML)

1 Tbsp (15 mL) Szechuan
    peppercorns
1 Tbsp (15 mL) fennel seeds
1 Tbsp (15 mL) whole clove buttons
1 Tbsp (15 mL) chopped
    cinnamon stick
1 Tbsp (15 mL) chopped whole
    star anise

In a dry skillet over medium heat, add the peppercorns, fennel, cloves, cinnamon, and star anise. Toss to warm through and heat until fragrant, about 1 minute. Transfer to a plate and allow to cool. Grind in a coffee or spice grinder and store in an airtight container for up to 2 months.

MUSHROOM CURRY POWDER

This is a versatile blend that works with potatoes and squash, and in soups and sauces. Buy fresh spices and use them up as soon as you can for the best results. Buy whole nutmeg and use a microplane grater to get the most amazing nutmeg flavor.

MAKES ABOUT 1½ CUPS (375 ML)

4 Tbsp (60 mL) cumin seeds

1 Tbsp (15 mL) black peppercorns

1 Tbsp (15 mL) coriander seeds

1 Tbsp (15 mL) chopped
    cinnamon stick

1 cup (250 mL) mushroom powder
    (porcini, button, shiitake, etc.)

1 Tbsp (15 mL) ground ginger

1 Tbsp (15 mL) ground turmeric

1 tsp (5 mL) freshly ground nutmeg

In a dry skillet over medium heat, add the cumin, peppercorns, coriander, and cinnamon. Shake the pan and heat until the mixture is aromatic, about 1 minute. Transfer to a plate and allow to cool. Grind in a coffee or spice grinder.

In a mixing bowl, place the mushroom powder, ginger, turmeric, nutmeg, and the ground spice blend. Mix well to blend and store in an airtight container for up to 2 months.

SPANISH SEASONING POWDER

This is a versatile rub that works with potatoes, many vegetables, sauces, and soups. When you add fresh garlic and a splash of olive oil, it approximates the flavors of chorizo sausage.

MAKES ABOUT ½ CUP (125 ML)

1 orange, zest only
2 Tbsp (30 mL) cumin seeds
1 Tbsp (15 mL) black peppercorns
1 Tbsp (15 mL) coriander seeds
1 Tbsp (15 mL) dried oregano
2 Tbsp (30 mL) hot Spanish paprika
1 Tbsp (15 mL) salt

Cover a small plate with paper towel. Place the orange zest on the paper and microwave for 30 seconds at a time until the zest is dry but not browned. (The time will depend on the power of the microwave.) The zest will stiffen as it cools. When it appears dry, remove it from the microwave and set aside until needed.

In a dry skillet over medium heat, add the cumin, peppercorns, and coriander. Shake the pan and heat until the mixture is aromatic, about 1 minute. Transfer to a plate and let cool. Grind in a coffee or spice grinder along with the orange zest and oregano.

In a mixing bowl, combine the ground spice mixture, paprika, and salt. Stir until the color of the mixture appears evenly distributed. Store in an airtight container for up to 2 months.

INFUSED OILS

Infused oils are great for finishing dishes with a splash of color and adding a burst of flavor. Spice blends work well to transfer the essence of the spice to a liquid. Gently heating the oil releases flavors and allows them to migrate to the oil. If you strain out the solids, you are left with delicately hued oil that is filled with intensity. It floats well on top of soups and the oil base helps to coat your taste buds with flavor.

MAKES ABOUT 1 CUP (250 ML)

1 cup (250 mL) grapeseed oil

2 Tbsp (30 mL) spice blend powder
(Five-Spice or Spanish Seasoning,
pages 81–85)

Heat a heavy-bottomed saucepan over low heat. Add the oil and whisk in the spice powder. Heat the oil gently to release the spice seasonings. Remove from the heat when warm and allow to infuse for about 15 minutes. Strain through a coffee filter (or line a strainer with an unbleached paper towel). Transfer the oil to a container with an airtight lid and store in the fridge for up to 1 month.

VARIATIONS:

- Fresh herbs: add ¼ cup (65 mL) chopped basil, rosemary, or mint to the oil. Infuse for 30 minutes. Purée with a hand blender, infuse overnight, and then strain.
- Fir needles: add ½ cup (125 mL) minced needles to the oil. Infuse for 15 minutes, purée with a hand blender, and strain until the oil is released (about 30 minutes).
- Dried mushrooms: add 2 Tbsp (30 mL) dried porcini, button, shiitake, or oyster mushrooms to the oil. Infuse for 1 hour and strain until the oil is released (about 30 minutes).
- Dried chilies: Add 2 Tbsp (30 mL) dried chili flakes to the oil and heat until hot (about 2 minutes). Remove from the heat and allow to cool to room temperature. You can strain the oil or leave the chilies in for texture and heat.
- Mushroom curry oil: Add 2 Tbsp (30mL) Mushroom Curry Powder (page 82) to the oil. Place over high heat and warm through for about 1 minute. You will see the curry color bloom in the oil. Remove from the heat and allow to cool.

STOCKS,
PURÉES,
AND
SAUCES

AROMATIC VEGETABLE STOCK

Roasting caramelizes the natural sugars in the vegetables and adds a depth of flavor to the stock. You can make a lighter and cleaner stock by skipping the roasting and omitting the soy sauce. This is the stock I call for in most of the recipes in this book. It can be made in a batch and frozen in 4 cup/1 L containers (I often recycle my yogurt containers). Feel free to substitute the other stock recipes in this chapter if you have them on hand or like the flavor combinations produced.

MAKES 16 CUPS (4 L)

2 cups (500 mL) chopped carrot

2 cups (500 mL) chopped onion

1 cup (250 mL) chopped celery

1 cup (250 mL) chopped fennel tops
(greens and leaves)

1 Tbsp (15 mL) minced garlic

2 Tbsp (30 mL) olive oil

Salt and pepper

1 Tbsp (15 mL) minced
rosemary leaves

1 Tbsp (15 mL) minced sage leaves

2 Tbsp (30 mL) minced celery leaves

2 Tbsp (30 mL) light soy sauce

Preheat the oven to 350°F/180°C.

In a roasting pan, mix together the carrot, onion, celery, and fennel tops. Sprinkle the garlic overtop and drizzle with the olive oil. Season well with salt and pepper and toss to coat. Place in the oven and roast until the vegetables just begin to brown, about 20 minutes. Remove from the oven and scrape the vegetables into a stockpot. Add about 1 cup (250 mL) of water to the roasting pan and scrape any browned bits into the stockpot. Add 15 cups (3¾ L) water along with the rosemary, sage, celery leaves, and soy. Bring to a boil then turn down the heat to a simmer and gently cook for about 1 hour.

Strain the stock and allow to cool to room temperature. Place in a large airtight container and refrigerate for up to 1 week.

CARAMELIZED ONION AND MUSHROOM STOCK

Onions have lots of natural sugars. Slow cooking caramelizes these sugars and creates an immense amount of flavor. Mushroom and caramel are also friends and create an intense umami hit.

MAKES 16 CUPS (4 L)

2 Tbsp (30 mL) olive oil

4 cups (1 L) sliced onions

2 cups (500 mL) chopped mushrooms
 (button, shiitake, oyster, etc.)

Salt and pepper

1 tsp (5 mL) honey

1 cup (250 mL) dry white wine

1 cup (250 mL) chopped celery

1 Tbsp (15 mL) minced garlic

1 Tbsp (15 mL) minced thyme leaves

1 Tbsp (15 mL) minced sage leaves

2 Tbsp (30 mL) minced celery leaves

In a large skillet over medium-high heat, add the olive oil and then the onion. Toss to coat the onion in the oil and add the mushrooms. Season well with salt and pepper. When the onion begins to brown, add the honey and toss to coat. When the honey begins to caramelize, add the wine. Toss the onion mixture to mix everything together and dissolve the caramel. When the wine is almost evaporated, remove from the heat and transfer to a stockpot.

Add about 1 cup (250 mL) water to the skillet and scrape any browned bits into the stockpot. Add 15 cups (3¾ L) water along with the celery, garlic, and thyme, sage, and celery leaves. Bring to a boil. Turn down the heat to a simmer and gently cook for about 1 hour.

Strain the stock and allow to cool to room temperature. Place it in a large airtight container and refrigerate for up to 1 week.

SMOKED CARROT DASHI

Dashi usually refers to a broth made with smoked bonito (or other dried smoked fish). This version uses smoked carrots to bring flavor and sweetness to the broth. In a pinch, grilled carrots would also work.

MAKES 16 CUPS (4 L)

2 lb (about 1 kg) cooled smoked
  carrots (see below)
1 (4-inch [10 cm]) square kombu
  (bull kelp)
2 Tbsp (30 mL) light miso paste
4 dried shiitake mushrooms
2 slices fresh ginger

Coarsely chop the carrots. Place them in a large stockpot and add 4 cups (1 L) water with the kombu, miso, dried shiitakes, and ginger. Bring to a slow boil over medium heat, turn down the heat to a simmer, and allow to gently cook for 30 minutes, or until the carrots are tender.

Drain the stock and retain the mushrooms for another use. Let cool to room temperature. Place in an airtight container and keep refrigerated for up to 1 week.

SMOKED CARROTS

2 lb (about 1 kg) carrots,
  peeled and trimmed
1 Tbsp (15 mL) olive oil
1 tsp (5 mL) honey
1 Tbsp (15 mL) Spanish Seasoning
  Powder (page 85)
1 tsp (5 mL) salt

Preheat the smoker to 150°F (65°C).

Place the carrots on a rimmed baking tray and drizzle with the olive oil and honey. Sprinkle the spice powder and salt overtop. Toss well to coat and allow to sit for 15 minutes, turning occasionally. Transfer to a cooling rack and allow to dry slightly. Transfer the rack to the smoker and cold-smoke for about 1 hour.

Remove from the heat and allow to cool before using.

MUSHROOM, VEGETABLE, AND MISO STOCK

Usually stock requires long cooking times, but miso broths and stocks are quick—
and packed full of flavor. Use this stock in place of the aromatic vegetable stock
listed in many of the recipes. I usually make this when I need a quick vegan broth.
The beer is optional and can be easily replaced with water.

MAKES 16 CUPS (4 L)

2 Tbsp (30 mL) olive oil

2 onions, peeled and sliced

2 Tbsp (30 mL) minced garlic

2 Tbsp (30 mL) minced ginger

2 cups (500 mL) chopped mushrooms
(button, shiitake, oyster, etc.)

1 cup (250 mL) chopped celery

2 carrots, peeled and chopped

2 Tbsp (30 mL) light miso paste

1 cup (250 mL) light-bodied beer
(lager or light ale) (optional)

In a stockpot over medium-high heat, add the olive oil, onion, garlic,
and ginger. Sauté until the onion softens and just begins to brown. Add
the mushrooms and stir to release the moisture and soften the mushrooms. Add the celery and carrots. Sauté until the vegetables begin to
brown and just start to stick to the bottom. Add the miso paste and stir
it into the vegetables. Add the beer (or 1 cup/250 mL water) and stir
to dissolve the miso and the browned bits on the bottom of the pot.
Add 16 cups (4 L) water, bring to a boil, and turn down the heat to a
simmer. Cook for about 1 hour, or until the vegetables are very soft.

Strain the stock and allow it to cool to room temperature. Place it
in a large airtight container and refrigerate for up to 1 week.

CORN COB STOCK

Make this stock after processing a batch of sweet corn. Boil the corn in a large pot of unsalted boiling water (16 cups/4 L) for about 10 minutes. Remove the corn, reserving the stock. Cut off the kernels and use them in a favorite recipe or vacuum-pack and freeze them.

MAKES 16 CUPS (4 L)

16 cups (4 L) reserved cooking water
   (from cooking corn)
1 cup (250 mL) dry white wine
12 cooked corn cobs
1 onion, peeled and diced
1 cup (250 mL) chopped celery
2 Tbsp (30 mL) celery leaves
¼ cup (65 mL) chopped
   cilantro stems
1 Tbsp (15 mL) minced garlic

In a large stockpot (it can be the same one you used to cook the corn), add the reserved cooking water, wine, cobs, onion, celery stalk and leaves, cilantro stems, and garlic. Bring to a boil. Turn down the heat to a simmer and gently cook for about 1 hour.

Strain the stock and allow it to cool to room temperature. Place it in a large airtight container and refrigerate for up to 1 week.

PEA AND MINT SAUCE

This recipe works equally well with fresh or frozen peas. It is a nice accompaniment to rice-, polenta-, or grain-based dishes. You can finish the sauce with a little cream, sour cream, or butter for a richer finish.

MAKES 4 CUPS (1 L)

2 cups (500 mL) Aromatic Vegetable
    Stock (page 90) or water
4 cups (1 L) shucked sweet peas
¼ cup (65 mL) dry white wine
2 Tbsp (30 mL) minced mint leaves
1 lemon, juice and zest
1 tsp (5 mL) honey
2 tsp (10 mL) tapioca starch
    (or cornstarch)
Salt and pepper

Place the stock in a saucepan over medium-high heat and bring to a boil. Add the peas and white wine and bring back to a boil. Cook for 2 to 3 minutes and add the mint, lemon juice and zest, and honey. Bring back to a boil and immediately purée with an immersion blender. Strain the mixture through a fine mesh sieve into another saucepan, pressing it with a small ladle or spoon to extract all the liquid.

Return to the heat and bring back to a boil. Mix the tapioca starch in a small bowl with 2 teaspoons (10 mL) water. Stir this into the sauce, a little at a time, until the mixture thickens. If you have added too much you can thin the sauce with a little more stock. If it is not thick enough for you, add a little more tapioca starch and water slurry. Season with salt and pepper to taste.

Remove from the heat and use immediately as a sauce. Any leftovers can be refrigerated in an airtight container for several days, but may have to be loosened with additional stock when being reheated. The sauce can be made in batches and then chilled and frozen, but may have to be thinned and re-blended when defrosted, as it tends to separate when thawed.

VEGETABLE AIOLI AND VARIATIONS

The reduction of vegetable juice adds a bright color and flavor to this aioli. The egg yolk adds a richness and gloss to the sauce that makes it wonderful for artistic designs and plating. If you want to magnify the garlic flavor, add a raw clove to the blender along with the egg yolk. The carrot aioli is also delicious with minced ginger in place of the garlic (just strain the juice about halfway through cooking, and then return to the pot to finish reducing). For the best results, juice your own carrots, but you can use storebought carrot juice in a pinch.

MAKES 1 CUP (250 ML)

4 cups (1 L) carrot juice
1 Tbsp (15 mL) minced garlic
1 tsp (5 mL) hot sauce
1 egg yolk
1 cup (250 mL) grapeseed oil
1 tsp (5 mL) lemon juice
Salt

In a heavy-bottomed saucepan, combine the carrot juice, garlic, and hot sauce. Bring to a boil, turn down the heat to a simmer, and reduce until only a thick liquid remains, about ¼ cup (65 mL). Watch carefully as the mixture will tend to stick and burn as it reduces. Lower the heat to a bare simmer as the liquid level decreases.

Remove from the heat and allow to cool slightly. Transfer to a blender (or use an immersion blender and a tall narrow container). Add the egg yolk to the hot liquid and pulse to blend. With the blender running, add the oil in a slow and steady stream. The more oil you add, the thicker the aioli will become. Stop the blender, add the lemon juice, and pulse quickly to mix. Season to taste with salt. Pulse again to blend. Use a spatula to remove the aioli from the blender. Place it in a small container with a tight-fitting lid and refrigerate until needed.

VARIATIONS (REPLACE CARROT JUICE WITH):
- Fresh beet juice: 4 cups (1 L)
- Fresh cucumber juice: 2 cups (500 mL)
- Cooked mushroom purée (cook out excess moisture): ½ cup (125 mL)
- Cooked spinach purée (squeeze out excess moisture before puréeing): ½ cup (125 mL)
- Cooked kale purée (squeeze out excess moisture before puréeing): ½ cup (125 mL)

CORN AND BLACK BEAN SAUCE

This strongly flavored sauce is great with a variety of grilled and steamed vegetables. It works very well to enliven a meal, particularly with a side of rice on the table. The corn adds a nice sweetness to the mix, but the sauce also works with broccoli, Asian vegetables, squash, or shredded leeks.

MAKES ABOUT 6 CUPS (1.5 L)

4 cups (1 L) Aromatic Vegetable Stock (page 90) or Corn Cob Stock (page 94) (or water)

2 cups (500 mL) uncooked corn kernels

2 Tbsp (30 mL) salted, fermented black beans, minced

1 onion, peeled, trimmed, and finely diced

1 red bell pepper, cored and finely diced

1 Tbsp (15 mL) minced ginger

1 Tbsp (15 mL) minced garlic

1 Tbsp (15 mL) soy sauce

1 tsp (5 mL) sesame oil

1 tsp (5 mL) hot sauce

1 Tbsp (15 mL) tapioca starch (or cornstarch)

2 Tbsp (30 mL) chopped cilantro leaves

Salt and pepper

Place the stock in a saucepan over medium-high heat and bring to a boil. Add the corn, black beans, onion, bell pepper, ginger, garlic, soy sauce, sesame oil, and hot sauce. Bring back to a boil, turn down the heat to a simmer and cook, uncovered, for 10 minutes, or until all the vegetables are soft.

Mix the tapioca starch in a small bowl with 1 tablespoon (15 mL) water. Stir this into the sauce, a little at a time, until the mixture thickens. If you have added too much you can thin the sauce with a little more stock. If it is not thick enough for you, add a little more tapioca starch and water slurry. Season with the cilantro leaves and salt and pepper to taste.

Remove from the heat and use immediately as a sauce. It can be refrigerated in an airtight container for several days, but may have to be loosened with additional stock when being reheated. This does not freeze well.

TOMATO AND BARLEY SAUCE

You can think of this as a vegetarian Bolognese sauce (traditionally made with ground meat). The barley gives texture, protein, and a toothsome bite to the sauce. Make a batch and keep it in the freezer for quick meals. I often make this with frozen blanched tomatoes, which have had their skins removed. This gives a smoother appearance to the sauce. Canned low-sodium stewed tomatoes also work well with this. I use a rice cooker to prepare the barley (1 cup/250 mL barley with 2 cups/500 mL water).

MAKES 4 CUPS (1 L)

2 Tbsp (30 mL) olive oil

2 onions, peeled, trimmed, and diced

2 cups (500 mL) mushrooms, cleaned and diced

2 cups (500 mL) diced celery

2 cups (500 mL) diced carrots

1 Tbsp (15 mL) minced garlic

10 cups (2.5 L) blanched tomatoes (about 5 lb/2.2 kg)

¼ cup (65 mL) shredded fresh basil

1 Tbsp (15 mL) hot sauce

2 cups (500 mL) cooked pearl barley

Salt and pepper

In a medium stockpot over medium-high heat, add the olive oil then the onions, mushrooms, celery, carrot, and garlic. Stir until the mixture starts to brown and begins to stick to the bottom of the pot. Add the blanched tomatoes and any accumulated juice. Stir to mix, bring to a boil, and then turn down the heat to a simmer. Cook, stirring occasionally, for 1 hour. Add the basil and hot sauce, and then the cooked barley. Stir to mix everything together, taste, and season with salt and pepper if necessary.

Simmer for 5 to 10 minutes to allow the barley to absorb some moisture and blend with the sauce. You can use this on pasta and polenta, and numerous other ways. Use immediately, or refrigerate in an airtight container for 3 to 4 days. It also freezes well for several months.

BEET, SOY, AND FIVE-SPICE PURÉE

This purée is bright, sweet, and intensely flavored. It works wonderfully as a base for grilled or steamed vegetables, as well as with raw foods like chopped fresh tomatoes topped with feta. The earthiness also pairs well with sautéed mushrooms.

MAKES 4 CUPS (I L)

4 lb (about 1.8 kg) whole red beets, topped and scrubbed

1 Tbsp (15 mL) Five-Spice Powder (page 81)

2 Tbsp (30 mL) butter (or coconut oil paste)

2 Tbsp (30 mL) chopped cilantro leaves

2 Tbsp (30 mL) light soy sauce

1 tsp (5 mL) sesame oil

Salt and pepper

Lemon or lime juice

In a large pot, place the beets and cover them with water. Place over high heat and bring to a boil. Turn down the heat and simmer for 20 to 30 minutes, or until the beets are easily pierced by a small knife. Drain and allow to cool enough to handle.

Peel and coarsely dice the warm beets. Place them in the bowl of a food processor and coarsely process. Add the butter, Five-Spice Powder, cilantro, soy sauce, and sesame oil. Purée until smooth. Taste, and season with salt (if needed) and a squeeze of lemon or lime juice to brighten the mixture. This can be made in advance and reheated before serving.

YAM PURÉE WITH SPANISH FLAVORS

This purée works nicely as a sauce for roasted or grilled vegetables and as a topping for bread. Yam has a high sugar content, so be careful when you roast it so that the sugars do not burn. I like to use a nice fleshy heirloom tomato like Roma or Bull's Heart for this dish.

MAKES ABOUT 4 CUPS (1 L)

4 cups (1 L) cubed, peeled yam

2 medium tomatoes,
    cored and chopped

6 cloves garlic, peeled

2 Tbsp (30 mL) olive oil

1 Tbsp (15 mL) Spanish Seasoning
    Powder (page 85)

1 cup (250 mL) cooked (or canned)
    chickpeas

Salt and pepper

Olive oil drizzle

Preheat the oven to 350°F (180°C).

On a rimmed baking tray, place the yam, tomatoes, and garlic cloves. Drizzle with the oil and sprinkle with the Spanish Seasoning Powder. Toss well to coat and place in the oven. Bake for 20 minutes, or until the yams are soft and beginning to brown. Remove from the oven and allow to cool.

Scrape the vegetables into the bowl of a food processor. Purée until smooth. Add the chickpeas. Pulse until smooth then process for 1 to 2 minutes until a very smooth purée is reached. Season with salt and pepper.

If the mixture is thick, add a drizzle of olive oil to smooth it out. If it is thin, add a few more chickpeas (or some cubes of bread) and purée to thicken the mixture (note: the thickness will depend on the type and ripeness of the tomato). Serve warm. This can be made ahead and refrigerated for 2 to 3 days. Reheat the purée prior to serving. I like to roast a whole head of garlic and reserve some of the cloves to garnish the top of the purée.

RAW

SHREDDED CARROT, DAIKON, PICKLED GINGER, AND SPROUTS

If you want to turn this into a spectacular salad, invest in a Japanese vegetable shredder (page 55). It turns a vegetable into an impossibly long string of curls. Place the shreds in a bath of water and ice cubes until just before you make the salad. The results will delight you.

SERVES 4

2 large carrots, peeled and trimmed

1 small daikon root,
    peeled and trimmed

1 Tbsp (15 mL) pickled ginger, cut in
    fine julienne

2 Tbsp (30 mL) rice vinegar

1 Tbsp (15 mL) honey

1 Tbsp (15 mL) light soy sauce

1 tsp (5 mL) sesame oil

2 Tbsp (30 mL) grapeseed oil

1 cup (250 mL) micro greens (or
    daikon sprouts or radish sprouts)

2 Tbsp (30 mL) toasted
    sunflower seeds

1 Tbsp (15 mL) shiso leaf (or Thai
    basil), shredded

1 Tbsp (15 mL) toasted sesame seeds

On a clean cutting board, shred the carrots and daikon with a grater or a Japanese shredder. Place in a bowl of cold water with a few ice cubes while you make the dressing.

In a salad bowl, combine the pickled ginger, rice vinegar, honey, soy sauce, and sesame oil. Whisk to mix, adding the grapeseed oil in a slow steady stream until incorporated. Drain the carrot and daikon. Shake the strainer and gently press the vegetables to remove any excess moisture (you can also place them in a salad spinner to do this). Add the micro greens, sunflower seeds, and shiso leaf. Toss to mix everything together and serve plated with a sprinkling of sesame seeds.

BEET AND APPLE SALAD WITH BASIL, LIME, AND HONEY

Beets have a wonderful crunch and earthiness that pairs well with the sweet crunch of apple. Use a red-skinned variety with a firm texture like Fuji for excellent results. This salad is great when the vegetables are cut in julienne or large batons. You can use a mandolin (page 52) to create an even, fine shred that adds a little elegance to the salad.

SERVES 4

1 lime, juice and zest

1 Tbsp (15 mL) honey

1 Tbsp (15 mL) yellow mustard

1 tsp (5 mL) hot sauce

2 Tbsp (30 mL) olive oil

1 large beet, peeled and trimmed

1 red apple, skin on, cored

2 Tbsp (30 mL) shredded fresh basil

Salt and pepper

Toasted pumpkin seeds, for garnish

Wedge of lime, for garnish

Basil leaves, for garnish

In a mixing bowl, combine the lime juice and zest, and honey. Whisk to dissolve the honey, then whisk in the mustard and hot sauce. Add the oil in a slow steady stream, whisking until incorporated.

On a clean cutting board, cut the beet into thin slices, then cut each slice into thin strips to form a julienne. Place in the dressing and toss to coat. Cut the apple, leaving the skin on, in the same manner. Add to the beet and toss to coat. Add the shredded basil, toss to mix, and season with salt and pepper. Transfer to a serving plate and garnish with toasted pumpkin seeds, a wedge of lime, basil leaves, and a final dusting of freshly ground black pepper.

TOMATO AND ARUGULA SALAD WITH PLUM DRESSING

This is a great dish for late summer when the heirloom tomatoes are ripe and many varieties are available. You can use any type of plum for the dressing. I use wild red plums from around the farm, but you could use black, red, or yellow plums with equally excellent results. The amount of vinegar needed for the dressing changes with the type and ripeness of the plums.

SERVES 4

Plum Dressing

1 cup (250 mL) chopped, pitted
     plums (skin on)
1 tsp (5 mL) minced ginger
2 Tbsp (30 mL) white wine vinegar
1 Tbsp (15 mL) olive oil
Salt and pepper

Salad

2 lb (about 1 kg) ripe tomatoes, cored
     and cut in wedges
4 cups (1 L) arugula leaves, washed
     and spun dry
1 green onion, trimmed and
     finely minced
Toasted sesame seeds, for garnish

Heat a saucepan over medium heat and add the plums, ginger, and vinegar. Cook until the plums release their moisture and begin to break down, about 5 minutes. Purée the mixture with an immersion blender and strain it into a mixing bowl, pressing down with a small ladle to extract all the juices from the pulp. Set aside to cool to room temperature.

Whisk in the olive oil and season with salt and pepper. Taste and adjust the seasoning (if necessary) with a little extra vinegar to make a balanced sweet and sour dressing.

In a mixing bowl, place the tomatoes and arugula. Drizzle with enough dressing to lightly cover the greens. Transfer to a serving plate, drizzle the extra sauce around the salad, and garnish with the green onion and sesame seeds. Serve immediately as this salad does not like to sit for very long.

HONEY-CURED GREEN TOMATOES
WITH HEMP SEED CRUMBLE

Green tomatoes usually overload the farm at the tail end of the season (here in the Pacific Northwest the season is never *quite* long enough). There are a few recipes in this book that turn the bounty into pure gold—this is one of them. Use whatever green tomatoes you have on hand, but the larger, meatier varieties tend to hold up better when cured.

SERVES 4

2 lb (about 1 kg) large
  green tomatoes
4 Tbsp (60 mL) honey
1 Tbsp (15 mL) salt
1 tsp (5 mL) pepper
2 Tbsp (30 mL) olive oil
1 Tbsp (15 mL) minced garlic
1 cup (250 mL) dried breadcrumbs
  (or panko)
¼ cup (65 mL) hemp seed hearts
1 Tbsp (15 mL) finely chopped fresh
  flat-leaf parsley
1 Tbsp (15 mL) freshly grated
  Parmesan cheese
Extra Parmesan cheese, for garnish

In a glass casserole dish, place a layer of tomatoes and drizzle them with the honey, salt, and pepper. Repeat with the remaining tomatoes and seasoning. Allow to sit for at least 1 hour, then gently turn the tomatoes to mix with the liquid. Marinate for an additional hour.

In a non-stick skillet over medium-high heat, place the olive oil and garlic. Heat until fragrant but not browned, about 1 minute. Add the breadcrumbs and stir to mix. Add the hemp seeds and parsley and toast until the crumbs just begin to brown. Transfer to a plate and allow to cool. Add the Parmesan cheese and toss to mix. Taste and adjust the seasoning with salt and pepper.

To serve, remove the tomatoes from the curing liquid and place them on a serving platter. Top with the hemp seed crumble and grate some additional Parmesan on top as a garnish. Serve at room temperature.

DAIKON, CUCUMBER, AND SEAWEED SALAD WITH LEMON, RAISINS, AND CAPERS

The mild radish flavor of daikon pairs nicely with the sweetness of the raisins and the saltiness of the capers and seaweed. The cucumber adds lightness and contrast to the mild funk of the daikon. Daikon is a vegetable that benefits from being cut into fine slivers. If you don't have the knife skills, try using a mandolin or Japanese vegetable shredder (page 55). If you make this salad ahead of time, add the seaweed garnish just before serving.

SERVES 4

1 lemon, juice and zest

¼ cup (65 mL) golden raisins, rinsed and chopped

1 Tbsp (15 mL) small caper berries, coarsely chopped

1 clove garlic, minced

2 Tbsp (30 mL) grapeseed oil

2 cups (500 mL) daikon, peeled and trimmed

1 English cucumber, split vertically, core removed

Salt and pepper

½ cup (125 mL) shredded nori seaweed

In a mixing bowl, combine the lemon juice and zest, raisins, capers, and garlic. Whisk to blend, adding the grapeseed oil in a slow, steady stream until incorporated. Set aside until needed.

On a cutting board, cut the daikon into thin rounds and then thin strips. Add to the dressing and toss to coat. Cut each side of cucumber into thin slices. Cut each slice into a thin strip and add to the daikon. Toss well to coat. Season to taste with salt and pepper. Place on a serving dish and garnish generously with shredded nori. Serve immediately.

SHREDDED KALE AND ROMAINE WITH SPICES

Rubbing the kale with salt and spices softens the texture and adds a punch of flavor to the salad. If you like stronger flavors, you can sprinkle some of the spice powder on top of the feta for appearance and additional intensity. Try to find goat feta if you can. Feta tends to be salty as it is packed in brine, so rinse the cheese before crumbling and don't add any additional salt to the salad.

SERVES 4–6

2 lb (about 1 kg) kale, washed and trimmed of stems

1 Tbsp (15 mL) Spanish Seasoning Powder (page 85)

1 tsp (5 mL) salt

2 Tbsp (30 mL) sherry vinegar

¼ cup (65 mL) green olives, pitted and minced

1 Tbsp (15 mL) finely minced shallots

1 tsp (5 mL) minced garlic

1 tsp (5 mL) hot sauce

2 Tbsp (30 mL) olive oil

1 head romaine lettuce, trimmed and washed

¼ cup (65 mL) crumbled feta cheese

On a cutting board, roll up a handful of kale leaves and cut them into a fine shred. Place them in a mixing bowl and repeat with the remaining kale. Sprinkle the spice mix on top along with the salt. With clean hands, rub the kale vigorously to bruise it and work the spice in with your hands. Set aside while you prepare the other ingredients.

In a salad bowl, place the vinegar with the olives, shallots, garlic, hot sauce, and 1 teaspoon (5 mL) water. Whisk to combine and then add the oil in a slow, steady stream, whisking until incorporated. Drain the kale and add it to the salad bowl. On a cutting board, remove any damaged outer leaves from the romaine and cut off the core. Chop the lettuce into thin rounds, starting at the base. Add to the salad mixture and toss to coat. Garnish with the crumbled feta. Serve at room temperature.

KOHLRABI SLAW WITH PUMPKIN SEED AND YOGURT PESTO

Kohlrabi adds a subtle spice and delicate crunch to this slaw. The pumpkin seed adds a nutty earthy tone that is balanced by the yogurt. I use thick, unsweetened Greek-style yogurt.

SERVES 4–6

1 cup (250 mL) toasted pumpkin
   seeds (plus extra for garnish)
1 tsp (5 mL) Mushroom Curry
   Powder (page 82)
   (or curry powder)
2 Tbsp (30 mL) yogurt
1 Tbsp (15 mL) honey
2 tsp (10 mL) sesame oil
1 clove garlic, minced
4 green onions, chopped coarsely
2 Tbsp (30 mL) chopped cilantro
2 Tbsp (30 mL) olive oil
4 cups (1 L) kohlrabi,
   peeled and shredded
2 cups (500 mL) shredded
   red cabbage
1 cup (250 mL) shredded carrot
Cilantro leaves, for garnish

In a food processor, place the pumpkin seeds, curry powder, yogurt, honey, sesame oil, garlic, green onions, and cilantro. Pulse until coarsely ground, pour in the olive oil, and process until relatively smooth but still with a bit of texture, about 1 minute.

In a salad bowl, place the kohlrabi, cabbage, and carrot. Add most of the pumpkin seed pesto, reserving ¼ cup (65 mL) for serving. Toss the vegetables to evenly coat them. Drizzle the extra pesto around the edges. Garnish with toasted pumpkin seeds and cilantro leaves. Serve at room temperature.

CABBAGE, PEANUT, AND CHILI SALAD

This is a chunky salad that packs a punch of flavor and spice. The type of chili used will greatly influence the heat level. Jalapeño is relatively mild, serrano a little spicier, and scotch bonnet peppers will kick it up to a lip-numbing intensity. Removing the seeds and membrane greatly reduces the heat level of the chili. If you like serious heat, add the minced whole chili (minus the stem).

SERVES 4–6

2 Tbsp (30 mL) peanut butter
    (crunchy or smooth)
1 Tbsp (15 mL) boiling or
    very hot water
1 Tbsp (15 mL) honey
1 Tbsp (15 mL) sesame oil
1 Tbsp (15 mL) light soy sauce
1 lime, juice and zest
1 chili pepper, seeded and
    finely minced
1 tsp (5 mL) Five-Spice Powder
    (page 81)
1 head green cabbage,
    cored and diced
1 carrot, peeled and thinly sliced
1 red, orange, or yellow bell pepper,
    cored and diced
1 red onion, peeled, trimmed,
    and minced
2 Tbsp (30 mL) shredded basil leaves
2 Tbsp (30 mL) shredded mint leaves
Salt and pepper
¼ cup (65 mL) dry-roasted peanuts,
    for garnish
Lime wedges, for garnish

In a small mixing bowl, combine the peanut butter and boiling water. Stir to mix and to dissolve the peanut butter. Add the honey, sesame oil, soy sauce, lime juice and zest, chili, and Five-Spice Powder and whisk to combine. Set aside until needed.

In a large mixing bowl, combine the cabbage, carrot, bell pepper, and red onion. Add the dressing to the vegetables and toss to coat. Just before serving, add the basil and mint and toss to coat. Taste, and season with salt and pepper if necessary. Transfer to a serving plate and top with dry-roasted peanuts and a lime wedge for garnish.

SOUPS

CHICKPEA SOUP WITH LIMA BEANS AND CORN

We use a lot of chickpeas around the farm. Often we soak the dried beans overnight and cook up a batch for soups and hummus. The cooked beans can be cooled, drained, and vacuum-packed before being frozen. They can be easily thawed out for quick use.

MAKES 8 CUPS (2 L)

8 cups (2 L) Aromatic Vegetable
    Stock (page 90) or Corn Cob
    Stock (page 94)
2 cups (500 mL) cooked (or canned)
    chickpeas
2 onions, peeled, trimmed, and diced
1 carrot, peeled, trimmed, and diced
1 cup (250 mL) diced celery
2 Tbsp (30 mL) minced fresh sage
2 Tbsp (30 mL) ground coriander
1 Tbsp (15 mL) minced garlic
2 cups (500 mL) uncooked
    corn kernels
2 cups (500 mL) cooked (or canned)
    lima beans
¼ cup (65 mL) sour cream
2 Tbsp (30 mL) finely minced
    green onion
Sweet paprika, for garnish

Heat a large stockpot over medium-high. Add the stock, chickpeas, onion, carrot, celery, sage, coriander, and garlic. Bring the soup to a boil, turn down the heat, and simmer for about 1 hour, or until the vegetables are very tender. Purée with an immersion blender until smooth.

Add the corn and lima beans. Bring back to a boil, turn down the heat, and simmer, uncovered, for 15 minutes, or until the beans are tender. Taste, and season with salt and pepper if necessary.

To serve, ladle the soup into a bowl, top with a spoonful of sour cream, and sprinkle with green onion and a pinch of sweet paprika. Serve immediately.

SMOKED BEET BORSCHT
WITH LEEK CRÈME FRAÎCHE

It may seem like a lot of work to smoke the beets but the reward is well worth it. The soup actually benefits from being chilled and refrigerated overnight, then reheated the next day. The thickness of the soup can be altered according to your taste. It can be a light broth or a thicker, hearty soup made by puréeing some of the vegetables (particularly the potato).

SERVES 6–8

1 lb (454 g) red beets,
    washed and scrubbed
16 cups (4 L) Aromatic Vegetable
    Stock (page 90) (or water)
4 large russet potatoes,
    peeled and diced
4 cups (1 L) shredded green cabbage
1 cup (250 mL) diced onion
1 cup (250 mL) shredded carrot
1 cup (250 mL) diced celery
2 Tbsp (30 mL) minced garlic
½ cup (125 mL) chopped fresh dill
Salt and pepper
1 Tbsp (15 mL) butter
1 cup (250 mL) leeks, washed and
    thinly sliced
½ cup (125 mL) white wine
1 cup (250 mL) crème fraîche
    (or sour cream)
Chopped dill leaves, for garnish

Preheat the smoker to 150°F (65°C).

In a large pot, place the beets and cover them with water. Place over high heat and bring to a boil. Turn down the heat and simmer for 20 to 30 minutes, or until the beets are easily pierced by a small knife. Drain and allow to cool enough to handle. Peel the beets and remove any rough edges from around the top. Cut into large rounds. Transfer to a cooling rack and allow to dry slightly. Transfer the rack to a smoker and cold-smoke for about 1 hour. Remove from the smoker and allow to cool.

Heat a large stockpot over medium-high heat. Add the stock, potatoes, cabbage, onion, carrot, and celery. Bring to a boil, turn down the heat to a simmer, and cook until the potatoes are just tender, about 10 minutes.

Chop the smoked beets into a fine dice and add to the pot along with the dill. Turn down the heat to a simmer and continue to cook for another 20 minutes to blend the flavors. Taste, and season with salt and pepper if necessary. To make a thicker-bodied soup, remove about 2 cups (500 mL) of the soup and purée it with an immersion blender. Return it to the soup and stir to incorporate. Keep warm until needed.

In a sauté pan over medium-high heat, melt the butter and add the leeks. Season with salt and pepper and sauté until the leeks just begin to brown. Add the white wine and reduce until almost all the liquid is evaporated. Remove from the heat and allow to cool. Place the leeks in a small bowl and add the crème fraîche. Stir to mix, taste, and season with salt and pepper if necessary.

To serve, ladle the soup into a bowl and top with a dollop of leek crème fraîche and a sprinkling of chopped dill leaves.

SPINACH AND BREAD SOUP WITH GARLIC CONFIT

You can make this soup as a purely vegetarian offering, but it is also wonderfully (and traditionally) made with a strong chicken stock in places like Spain and Portugal. They might even add a poached egg to top the finished bowl of soup. My version uses caramelized onion stock with excellent results. Feel free to add more garlic to the mix and to substitute kale or stinging nettles for the spinach. Rustic white bread or baguette gives the nicest texture, but your favorite whole grain bread will also give good results.

SERVES 6–8

1 head garlic, peeled into cloves
   (skin removed)
¼ cup (65 mL) olive oil
1 Tbsp (15 mL) fresh rosemary
   leaves, chopped
16 cups (4 L) Aromatic Vegetable
   Stock (page 90) (or water)
1 cup (250 mL) diced celery
2 Tbsp (30 mL) minced garlic
1 lb (454 g) spinach, washed and
   stems removed
2 cups (500 mL) cubed bread
Salt and pepper

Preheat the oven to 350°F (180°C).

In a small ovenproof saucepan, place the peeled garlic and cover it with the olive oil. Bring to a slow simmer, stirring to coat the garlic, then add the rosemary and mix it into the oil. Transfer to the hot oven and cook for 10 minutes, stirring occasionally. The garlic will brown slightly and be soft to the touch when cooked. Remove from the oven and allow to cool in the oil in the pan.

Heat a large stockpot over medium-high heat. Add the stock, celery, and minced garlic, bring to a boil, turn down the heat, and simmer 10–15 minutes, or until the celery is soft. Add the spinach and stir until wilted, 1 to 2 minutes. Purée the soup with an immersion blender until smooth and bright green. Add the bread cubes and stir gently to mix. Taste, and season with salt and pepper if necessary.

To serve, ladle into a soup bowl and top with a few caramelized garlic cloves and a healthy drizzle of the garlic-infused olive oil. Serve immediately.

CORN, SWEET POTATO, AND MISO CHOWDER

This soup is tasty with fresh or frozen corn. If you like heat, feel free to add chilies or hot sauce. This is also a soup that can be finished with a little cream or sour cream for a smoother, richer finish. If you are pulling out all the stops you could add 1 teaspoon (5 mL) of truffle paste or good truffle oil.

SERVES 6–8

1 Tbsp (15 mL) grapeseed oil

4 cups (1 L) uncooked corn kernels

2 cups (500 mL) diced peeled
    sweet potato

1 cup (250 mL) diced onion

1 cup (250 mL) diced carrot

1 cup (250 mL) diced celery

2 Tbsp (30 mL) minced garlic

2 Tbsp (30 mL) light miso paste

1 Tbsp (15 mL) Spanish Seasoning
    Powder (page 85)

16 cups (4 L) Corn Cob Stock
    (page 94) (or water)

¼ cup (65 mL) tapioca starch
    (or cornstarch)

2 Tbsp (30 mL) chopped cilantro or
    basil, for garnish

Heat a large stockpot over medium-high heat. Add the oil then the corn, sweet potato, onion, carrot, celery, garlic, miso paste, and spice powder. Sauté until the onion softens and just begins to brown.

Add the stock and bring the soup to a boil. Turn down the heat to a simmer and cook until the vegetables are tender, about 30 minutes.

Mix the tapioca starch in a small bowl with enough water (about 2 tsp/10 mL) to make a paste. Stir this into the soup a little at a time, stirring constantly until it is mixed in and the soup thickens slightly. Ladle into a bowl and garnish with a sprinkle of cilantro or basil.

This soup is best when made a day in advance, cooled, and reheated to order.

SQUASH SOUP WITH COCONUT MILK, MUSHROOM CURRY OIL, AND HAZELNUTS

Use a dark-fleshed squash like kabocha or kuri for the best results. Other firm types like acorn or butternut also make beautiful puréed soups. The spice mix gives it a gentle heat, but feel free to add chilies or hot sauce to bump up the heat level.

SERVES 6–8

1 medium squash (2 lb/about 1 kg)

2 Tbsp (30 mL) olive oil

Salt and pepper

1 Tbsp (15 mL) grapeseed oil

1 cup (250 mL) diced onion

1 cup (250 mL) shredded carrot

1 cup (250 mL) diced celery

2 Tbsp (30 mL) minced garlic

2 Tbsp (30 mL) minced ginger

2 Tbsp (30 mL) Mushroom Curry
    Powder (page 82)

1 tsp (5 mL) hot sauce

12 cups (3 L) Aromatic Vegetable
    Stock (page 90) (or water)

2 cups (500 mL) coconut milk

½ cup (125 mL) chopped cilantro

2 Tbsp (30 mL) Mushroom Curry Oil
    (page 86)

2 Tbsp (30 mL) chopped, toasted
    hazelnuts (optional)

Preheat the oven to 350°F (180°C).

Cut the squash in half lengthwise and remove the seeds and membrane. Cut each half lengthwise into four slices and place them on a rimmed baking tray. Drizzle with the olive oil and season with salt and pepper. Place in the oven and roast until tender and just beginning to brown, about 30 minutes. Remove from the oven and allow to cool on a rack. When cool enough to handle, peel off and discard the skin.

In a stockpot over medium-high heat, place the grapeseed oil then the onion, carrot, celery, garlic, ginger, curry powder, and hot sauce. Stir to mix and sauté for 1 to 2 minutes, or until the mix is fragrant and just beginning to stick to the bottom of the pot. Add the stock, coconut milk, and cilantro. Stir to mix everything together, bring to a boil, then simmer for about 30 minutes, or until the vegetables are very tender. Purée with an immersion blender until very smooth. Strain into a container through a fine mesh sieve, pressing down and rubbing with a ladle to extract all the liquid. Return the strained soup to the pot and bring back to a boil for at least 2 minutes to warm through.

To serve, ladle hot soup into a bowl, drizzle with Mushroom Curry Oil, and sprinkle with chopped hazelnuts.

FIVE-SPICE TOMATO SOUP WITH CRISPY RICE

Freshly prepared spices elevate this soup to the sublime, particularly if you use ripe field tomatoes in season. This dish is inspired by a Chinese technique called singing rice where compressed rice is deep-fried until crispy and very hot, then sauce is poured on top of the rice, and the dish sizzles and pops as it is served. Cook 1 cup (250 mL) of short-grain rice with 2 cups (500 mL) of water to prepare the rice. Simmer, covered, for 20 minutes and set aside to cool.

SERVES 6–8

4 lb (1.8 kg) ripe tomatoes, cored and roughly chopped

4 cups (1 L) Aromatic Vegetable Stock (page 90) (or water)

1 cup (250 mL) diced onion

1 cup (250 mL) diced celery

2 Tbsp (30 mL) minced garlic

1 Tbsp (15 mL) Five-Spice Powder (page 81)

½ cup (125 mL) chopped basil leaves

1 tsp (5 mL) hot sauce

Salt and pepper

2 cups (500 mL) cooked short-grain rice

2 Tbsp (30 mL) grapeseed oil

2 Tbsp (30 mL) tapioca starch (or cornstarch)

2 green onions, finely minced

1 Tbsp (15 mL) toasted sesame seeds

Heat a large stockpot over medium-high heat. Add the tomatoes, stock, onion, celery, garlic, and Five-Spice Powder. Bring to a boil and then turn down the heat to a simmer. Simmer the soup for 1 hour, or until the tomato starts to break down. Purée with an immersion blender until smooth then strain it into a container through a fine mesh sieve, pressing with a ladle to remove all the liquid and leaving only skin and seeds behind. Return to the stockpot and bring back to a boil. Add the basil, taste, and season with hot sauce, salt, and pepper. Depending on the ripeness of the tomatoes, you may want to add 1 tablespoon (15 mL) of honey to the soup. It should have a nice sweet flavor. Keep warm until needed.

Preheat the oven to 350°F (180°C).

Drizzle the bottom of a rimmed baking tray with 1 tablespoon (15 mL) of the grapeseed oil. Place the cooked rice on the tray and pat it with your hands to form an even layer. Drizzle the remaining oil overtop and smooth it over the rice. Season with salt and pepper, place in the oven, and bake for 20 to 30 minutes, or until the rice is lightly browned on top. Break up the rice into bite-size chunks.

Bring the soup back to a boil. Mix the tapioca starch in a small bowl with enough water (about 2 tsp / 10mL) to make a thin paste and pour it into the boiling soup. Stir to blend and slightly thicken the sauce. Ladle into a serving bowl and crumble a generous amount of baked rice overtop. Garnish with green onions and sesame seeds. Serve immediately.

CARROT SOUP WITH CINNAMON AND COUSCOUS

Morocco is the inspiration for this soup. You will be rewarded for seeking out the freshest cinnamon stick you can find. Fresh cinnamon has a menthol-like (tingling) quality that dissipates over time. You can substitute 1 tablespoon (15 mL) Five-Spice Powder, Mushroom Curry Powder, or Spanish Seasoning Powder (pages 81–85) with good results. If you want to avoid wheat, make this soup with cooked quinoa in place of the couscous. Adding the couscous at the end produces a wonderful chewy texture.

SERVES 6–8

2 cups (500 mL) couscous

4 cups (1 L) boiling water

1 Tbsp (15 mL) grapeseed oil

8 cups (2 L) chopped carrots

1 cup (250 mL) diced onion

1 cup (250 mL) diced celery

2 Tbsp (30 mL) minced garlic

2 Tbsp (30 mL) minced ginger

2 sticks cinnamon, chopped

16 cups (4 L) Aromatic Vegetable
 Stock (page 90) (or water)

1 russet potato, peeled and diced

¼ cup (65 mL) plain yogurt

1 lime, juice and zest

1 tsp (5 mL) honey

In a heatproof bowl, combine the couscous with the boiling water. Let it sit for at least 15 minutes, stirring occasionally. Keep warm.

Heat a large stockpot over medium-high heat. Add the oil then the carrots, onion, celery, garlic, ginger, and cinnamon. Sauté until the vegetables soften and just begin to brown. Add the stock and potato. Bring to a boil, turn down the heat to a simmer, and cook for 30 minutes, or until the vegetables are cooked and soft. Purée with an immersion blender until the soup is very smooth. Strain into a container through a fine mesh sieve, pressing down and rubbing the pulp with a ladle to extract all the liquid. Return the soup to the stockpot. Taste, and season with salt and pepper if necessary.

In a small bowl, mix together the yogurt, lime juice and zest, and honey. If necessary, thin the mixture with a little water until a pouring consistency is reached.

To serve, place a heap of warm couscous in the bowl and ladle the hot soup on top. Garnish with a drizzle of the yogurt mixture.

BAKING,
FLATBREADS,
AND
PANCAKES

YAM FLATBREAD

Yam adds a wonderful color and sweetness to this bread, but be careful with the increased level of sugar it also brings, as the surface may brown quickly. The onions should be charred, and the bread will sound hollow when tapped. Roast the yams in a hot (350°F/180°C) oven for 30 minutes. Let cool and remove the flesh from the skin. You will need about 3 medium yams to make 2 cups (500 mL) of mash.

MAKES 1 LARGE FLAT LOAF

1 Tbsp (15 mL) instant yeast

2 cups (500 mL) warm water
  (about 120°F/49°C)

1 tsp (5 mL) honey

6 cups (1.5 L) unbleached bread flour

2 cups (500 mL) cooked mashed yams

1 tsp (5 mL) salt

2 Tbsp (30 mL) olive oil

2 Tbsp (30 mL) chopped
  fresh rosemary

1 onion, peeled, trimmed,
  and thinly sliced

1 Tbsp (15 mL) coarse sea salt

In a small bowl, combine the yeast with the warm water and honey. Allow to sit for 5 minutes to activate the yeast.

In the bowl of a mixer fitted with a dough hook, place the flour, mashed yam, and salt. Add half the yeast mixture and process on medium speed. Clean the sides of the bowl with a spatula and keep adding the rest of the yeast mixture (with the mixer running) until a soft, moist dough is formed. You may not need all the flour, or you may have to add some additional water. If the dough ball appears sticky, add a spoonful of flour at a time until the surface is smooth and does not stick to the bowl.

Transfer the dough to a clean, floured surface and knead the dough until it has a smooth texture. Return the dough to the mixer bowl and cover with a clean, dry kitchen towel. Let the dough sit in a warm, draft-free spot for about 1 hour. Transfer the dough to a floured cutting board, dust it with flour, and roll it out to a rectangle shape. Place the dough on a roasting pan lined with parchment paper and spread it out to completely cover the sheet. Cover with the towel again and let sit to rise a second time, about 1 hour.

Once the dough has risen, preheat the oven to 400°F (200°C). Prod the dough with your fingers to dimple the entire surface. Brush with the olive oil and sprinkle with the rosemary and onion slices. Season well with coarse sea salt. Place in the oven and bake for 30 minutes, or until the dough is golden brown and the onion slices are slightly charred. Remove from the oven and cool on a wire rack for a few minutes before cutting.

SHREDDED VEGETABLE PANCAKES

These pancakes are similar to the Japanese okonomiyaki vegetable cakes. They can be served with soy sauce as an appetizer or topped with an egg for an excellent breakfast treat. They are also wonderful as a main course topped with a vegetable-based sauce (see pages 95–99).

SERVES 4–6

1 red bell pepper, cored and cut in julienne

1 carrot, peeled and cut in julienne

1 leek, trimmed, washed, and shredded

1 cup (250 mL) shredded cooking greens (kale, mustard, bok choy, etc.)

4 eggs, lightly beaten

1 cup (250 mL) all-purpose flour

1 Tbsp (15 mL) Mushroom Curry Powder (page 82)

1 Tbsp (15 mL) sesame seeds

½ tsp (2.5 mL) baking powder

2 Tbsp (30 mL) vegetable oil (more if needed)

Salt and pepper

In a mixing bowl, combine the pepper, carrot, leek, and greens. Toss to mix. Add the eggs and stir well to coat. In a small bowl, combine the flour, curry powder, sesame seeds, and baking powder. Add this to the vegetable mixture and stir quickly to coat. Season well with salt and pepper.

Preheat the oven to 250°F (120°C).

Place a large non-stick skillet over medium-high heat and add a light coating of the vegetable oil. For each pancake, spoon about ¼ cup (65 mL) of the mixture into the pan, pressing down lightly with a fork to flatten it. Make four pancakes at a time, leaving about 1 inch (2.5 cm) between pancakes.

Fry until golden brown, crispy on the outside, and cooked through, 5 to 6 minutes per side. If the pancake starts to scorch (burn), turn down the heat to medium or medium-low. Transfer the cooked pancakes to a baking sheet lined with paper towel and place them in the oven to keep warm. Repeat with the remaining batter and oil. Serve warm.

SESAME BUNS WITH LEEKS AND GARLIC

These delicious buns make a great side for any of the soups in this book. They tend to be best when fresh, but can be reheated in the oven the next day. You can use whole grain flour (or a blend) with good results, but you may have to add a bit more water to achieve a nice soft and pliable dough.

MAKES 12 BUNS

2 tsp (10 mL) instant yeast

1 cup (250 mL) warm water (about 120°F/49°C)

1 tsp (5 mL) honey

2 Tbsp (30 mL) grapeseed oil

1 cup (250 mL) sliced leeks

2 Tbsp (30 mL) minced garlic

Salt and pepper

3 cups (750 mL) unbleached bread flour

1 tsp (5 mL) salt

1 Tbsp (15 mL) coarse sea salt

1 egg, beaten

1 Tbsp (15 mL) sesame seeds

In a small bowl, combine the yeast with the warm water and honey. Allow to sit for 5 minutes to activate the yeast.

In a sauté pan over medium-high heat, add the oil then the leeks and garlic. Season to taste with salt and pepper and sauté until the moisture evaporates and the leeks just begin to brown. Allow to cool.

In the bowl of a mixer fitted with a dough hook, place the flour and salt. Add half the yeast mixture and process on medium speed. Clean the sides of the bowl with a spatula and keep adding the rest of the yeast mixture (with the mixer running) until a soft and moist dough is formed. You may not need all the flour, or you may have to add some additional water if the dough appears dry or firm. Add the leeks and process until just incorporated. If the dough ball appears sticky, add a spoonful of flour at a time until the surface is smooth and does not stick to the bowl.

Transfer the dough to a clean, floured surface and knead until a smooth texture is developed. Return the dough to the mixer bowl and cover with a clean, dry kitchen towel. Let the dough sit in a warm, draft-free spot for about 1 hour. Transfer the dough to a floured cutting board, dust it with flour, and cut it into four equal pieces. Roll each piece into a log and cut each log into three pieces. Roll each chunk into a ball. Place on a roasting pan lined with parchment paper, cover with the towel, and let sit for 20 minutes to rest.

After the dough has slightly risen and appears to be plump, brush with beaten egg and sprinkle with sesame seeds. Allow to rest for an additional 20 minutes.

Once the dough has risen and springs back lightly to the touch, preheat the oven to 400°F (200°C). Place the roasting pan with the dough balls in the oven and bake for 20 minutes, or until the dough has risen and is golden brown. If you tap a bun with your finger it should sound hollow; the crust should be firm and well browned. Remove from the oven and let cool on a rack. Serve warm.

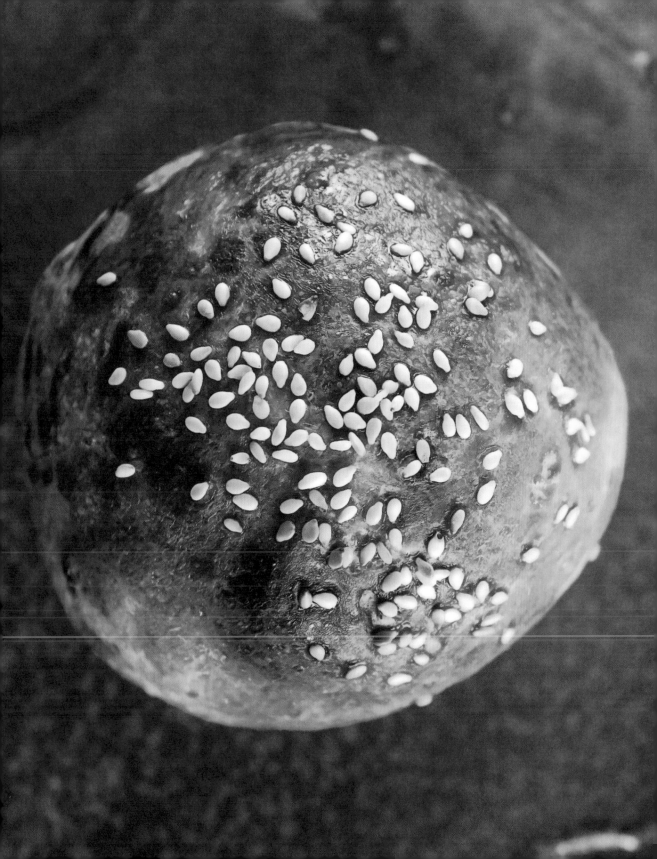

ROTI STUFFED WITH ROASTED BUTTERNUT SQUASH AND ONION MASH

A roti is an Indian flatbread, not unlike a flour tortilla (which you can substitute for the roti). Rotis are easy to make and can be made in batches and frozen. You can also cook rotis directly on a barbecue grill. The char and smoke of the grill adds an effect similar to the one produced by the traditional tandoori oven used to cook roti.

SERVES 4–6

2 cups (500 mL) all-purpose flour

1 tsp (5 mL) salt

¾ cup (190 mL) hot water
  (120°F/49°C)

1 Tbsp (15 mL) melted butter
  (or olive oil)

2 cups (500 mL) cubed butternut
  squash (flesh only,
  peeled and seeded)

1 onion, peeled, trimmed, and sliced

1 Tbsp (15 mL) Mushroom Curry
  Powder (page 82)

1 Tbsp (15 mL) olive oil

Salt and pepper

2 Tbsp (30 mL) grapeseed oil

In a mixer fitted with a dough hook, combine the flour and salt. With the machine running, add the water in a steady stream, followed by the melted butter. Knead on low speed for 4 to 5 minutes, or until the dough comes together. You may not need all the flour, or you may have to add some additional water if the dough appears dry or firm. If the dough ball appears sticky, add a spoonful of flour at a time until the surface is smooth and does not stick to the bowl. Remove the dough from the machine, place it on a well-floured work surface, and knead until the dough is smooth and soft. Cover with a clean, dry towel and let rest for 30 minutes.

Preheat the oven to 350°F (180°C).

On a rimmed baking tray, mix together the squash, onion, Mushroom Curry Powder, and olive oil. Season well with salt and pepper. Place in the oven and roast for about 20 minutes, or until the squash is soft and browned. Transfer to a food processor and pulse to a coarse paste.

On a clean, floured work surface, roll the dough into a long 2-inch (5 cm) wide rope. Cut into 1-inch (2.5 cm) chunks. Take one piece, dust it with flour, and roll it out into a thin circle, about 6 inches (15 cm) in diameter. Repeat with the remaining dough. You should end up with about 12 circles of dough. Brush the edge of one round with water and smear the squash filling over the centre, being careful not to coat the edge. Top with a second round of dough and press down with your fingers to secure the edge. Repeat with the remaining dough and filling.

Heat a skillet (or cast iron griddle) over medium heat and drizzle a little grapeseed oil in the pan. Add the roti and cook until the bottom is browned and beginning to color, 1 to 2 minutes. Carefully flip and cook the other side. Transfer to a plate and place in the oven to keep warm. Repeat with the remaining rotis. Serve warm.

BASIC FLAKY PIE DOUGH WITH VARIATIONS

This is a versatile pie dough that works well for desserts or savory pies. Mixing gently to bring the dough just together makes a very tender and flaky pastry.

MAKES 4 PORTIONS, OR ENOUGH DOUGH FOR 4 SINGLE-CRUST 10-INCH (25 CM) PIES

5½ cups (1.375 L) all-purpose flour

2 tsp (10 mL) salt

1 lb (454 g) lard or vegetable
    shortening

1 egg

1 Tbsp (15 mL) vinegar

In a mixing bowl, stir together the flour and salt. Cut the lard or shortening into rough cubes and toss them in the flour. Cut in the lard using a pastry cutter or two knives until the mixture resembles pea-sized lumps. In a bowl, beat the egg with a fork. Add the vinegar and enough cold water to make 1 cup (250 mL). Stir the liquid into the flour mixture until incorporated and the dough starts to come together. Gently knead until the mixture just comes together in a ball. Divide the dough into four portions. Cover each portion with plastic wrap and refrigerate for at least 1 hour.

When ready to proceed, roll out the dough on a floured work surface, using a good dusting of flour on the dough and the rolling pin. Proceed with the directions in the pie recipe. The dough can also be frozen for up to 1 month.

VARIATIONS (ADD WITH THE FLOUR):

- Cheddar and green onion dough: add 1 cup (250 mL) shredded aged cheddar and 4 green onions, trimmed and minced
- Herb dough: add 2 Tbsp (30 mL) minced fresh rosemary, sage, or thyme
- Sesame seed dough: add ¼ cup (65 mL) sesame seeds
- Black pepper dough: add 1 Tbsp (15 mL) freshly ground black pepper
- Turmeric dough: add 1 Tbsp (15 mL) ground turmeric

CARAMELIZED MAPLE AND TOMATO TARTE TATIN WITH GOAT CHEESE SAUCE

This tart works with many types of tomatoes. You could use large tomatoes or cherry tomatoes with equally good results. In season, you can also use a variety of colors like red, green, white, and purple varieties. Out of season, you can use local hothouse tomatoes. This tart is best eaten the day it is made. Reheat it in a warm oven if it has cooled.

SERVES 4–6

2 Tbsp (30 mL) maple syrup

1 tsp (5 mL) pepper

4 large tomatoes, cored and
  sliced thickly

Salt

2 Tbsp (30 mL) minced fresh basil

1 Tbsp (15 mL) minced garlic

¼ recipe Basic Flaky Pie Dough
  (page 137)

All-purpose flour for rolling
  the dough

¼ cup (65 mL) goat cheese

2 Tbsp (30 mL) whipping cream
  or milk

Preheat the oven to 350°F (180°C).

Place a casserole dish (13- × 9-inch / 33 × 23 cm) on a work surface. Cut a piece of parchment paper to overlap the dish by about 2 inches (5 cm). Split each corner with a pair of scissors to a depth of 2 inches (5 cm). Oil the casserole dish and press the parchment into the dish. The corners will fold over to evenly cover the bottom and sides of the dish.

Drizzle the bottom of the parchment with the maple syrup and pepper. Layer the tomatoes to evenly cover the parchment (overlapping is fine). Sprinkle with salt and more pepper and basil. Flour a work surface and place the pastry on the surface, dust it well with flour, and roll it out to be slightly larger than the casserole dish. Lay the pastry on top of the tomatoes and gently press into them. Cut off any excess pastry to evenly fit it into the casserole dish.

Place the casserole in the oven and bake until the pastry is golden brown and the filling is bubbling around the sides, about 30 minutes. Remove from the oven and let cool on a wire rack. In a small bowl, combine the goat cheese and cream. Whisk until smooth.

When the pastry has reached room temperature, place a clean cutting board on top. Place one hand under the casserole and one hand firmly on the cutting board. Quickly flip the tart so the cutting board is on the bottom. Lift the casserole dish, tapping it gently if it does not release. Remove the parchment and smooth out any tomatoes that have been jostled out of place.

Cut into rectangles, place on a serving plate, and drizzle with the goat cheese mixture. Serve hot (reheat in the oven) or warm.

CURRIED MUSHROOM AND ROOT VEGETABLE PIE

You can also make this pie with a top and bottom crust, in which case you will need double the dough specified in the recipe. Feel free to substitute other vegetables into the mix. Cauliflower, broccoli, sweet peas, corn, and squash are all good additions.

SERVES 6–8

1 Tbsp (15 mL) grapeseed oil

1 large onion, chopped

2 cups (500 mL) chopped mushrooms
   (button, oyster, chanterelle, etc.)

2 Tbsp (30 mL) Mushroom Curry
   Powder (page 82) or
   mild curry powder

1 Tbsp (15 mL) salt

1 Tbsp (15 mL) chopped garlic

2 cups (500 mL) peeled, diced potato

2 cups (500 mL) peeled, diced carrots

2 cups (500 mL) peeled, diced turnip

2 cups (500 mL) peeled, diced parsnip

4 cups (1 L) Aromatic Vegetable
   Stock (page 90) or water

¼ cup (65 mL) chopped cilantro or
   mustard greens

1 Tbsp (15 mL) hot sauce

Salt and pepper

2 Tbsp (30 mL) tapioca starch
   (or cornstarch)

¼ recipe Basic Flaky Pie Dough
   (page 137)

All-purpose flour for rolling
   the dough

1 egg, beaten

1 tsp (5 mL) cumin seeds

Warm a large saucepan over medium-high heat and add the oil then the onion. Sauté until the onion begins to soften and slightly brown. Add the mushrooms, Mushroom Curry Powder, salt, and garlic. Sauté until the mushrooms release their moisture, the moisture evaporates, and the contents begin to stick to the bottom of the pan. Add the potato, carrot, turnip, and parsnip. Cover with the stock, bring to a boil, turn down the heat to a simmer, and cook for 20 minutes, or until the vegetables are just tender. Season with the cilantro, hot sauce, salt, and pepper. Mix the tapioca starch with a little cold water to make a thin paste. Stir this into the simmering liquid until the sauce thickens. Transfer to a casserole dish (13- × 9-inch/33 × 23 cm) and allow to cool slightly.

Flour a work surface and place the pastry on the surface, dust it well with flour, and roll it out to be slightly larger than the casserole dish. Lay the pastry on top of the vegetables and gently press into them. Cut off any excess pastry to evenly fit it into the casserole dish. Cut two or three short slits in the top to allow steam to vent. Brush with the beaten egg and sprinkle lightly with the cumin seeds.

Place the casserole in the oven and bake until the pastry is golden brown and the filling is bubbling around the sides, about 30 minutes. Remove from the oven and let cool on a wire rack. Serve warm.

POTATO TART WITH CHEDDAR AND GREEN ONION PASTRY

Russet potatoes have a soft texture and enough starch to hold this delicious potato tart together. This dish would make a nice appetizer and also makes a great dinner or lunch with a side salad. Lots of cheese types work with this dish. Nutty cheeses like Gruyère or aged Gouda work well with the richness of the potato and cream. Blue cheeses like Stilton and Gorgonzola are very nice as contrasting flavors to the potatoes.

SERVES 6–8

1 cup (250 mL) whipping cream (or milk)

1 Tbsp (15 mL) chopped fresh rosemary

1 Tbsp (15 mL) chopped fresh sage

1 Tbsp (15 mL) chopped garlic

1 tsp (5 mL) freshly grated nutmeg

Salt and pepper

¼ recipe Cheddar and Green Onion Pie Dough (page 137)

4 large russet potatoes

1 cup (250 mL) grated white cheddar or Gruyère cheese

Additional grated cheese, for topping

4 green onions, trimmed and minced

In a saucepan, combine the cream, rosemary, sage, and garlic. Season well with nutmeg, salt, and pepper. Place the saucepan over medium-high heat and bring to a boil. The cream will immediately foam so be ready to pull it off the heat quickly. Remove from the heat and allow to infuse for 15 minutes.

Flour a clean work surface and place the pastry on top. Dust the pastry well with flour and roll it out to be slightly larger than a large pie plate (9-inch/23 cm). Gently fold the pastry and drape it on top of the pie plate, unfolding it onto the bottom. Gently press with your fingers to form the pastry to the bottom and side of the dish. Leaving about 1 inch (2.5 cm) of pastry as an overlap, cut off any excess pastry around the edges. Refrigerate to chill for at least 15 minutes.

Preheat the oven to 350°F (180°C).

Peel the potatoes and rinse them in cold water. Use a mandolin (page 52), or a very sharp knife, to cut the potato into very thin slices. Place a layer of potatoes on the bottom of the pastry. Cover with infused cream mixture and a very light sprinkling of grated cheese. Repeat with the remaining potato and cream until you reach the top of the crust. Press down gently with your hand to compress the final layer of potato. Pour over the remaining liquid and sprinkle with a little of the cheese and the green onion.

Place in the oven and bake until the potato is cooked through and the top is browned, about 1 hour. Test with a small sharp knife: it will easily penetrate the potato with no resistance when cooked through. Remove from the oven and let cool on a wire rack.

The tart can be eaten immediately, but it is even better if allowed to sit overnight to set up. In this case, allow the tart to cool completely then refrigerate overnight. Cut into wedges when cold. To serve the chilled tart, place the wedges on a baking tray, place them in a 350°F (180°C) oven, and bake until warmed through and the edges are slightly browned.

SWEET POTATO BLINIS WITH FIVE-SPICE TOMATO JAM

The sweet potato in this recipe can be boiled, steamed, or baked (before baking, toss it with a little olive oil). You have to work quickly with raw sweet potato because as soon as it is peeled and chopped, it begins to oxidize, quickly turning an unappetizing grey. As soon as you have chopped it up, put it in liquid or start to cook it immediately. It also has a high sugar content, so if you roast it, check on it every 5 minutes or so, until it's soft and starting to brown. It takes about 3 medium sweet potatoes to make 2 cups (500 mL) cooked. Mash the cooked sweet potato or process it lightly in a food processor before continuing.

SERVES 4–6

2 cups (500 mL) cooked sweet
    potato, mashed
2 eggs, lightly beaten
1 cup (250 mL) all-purpose (or
    buckwheat) flour
1 tsp (5 mL) baking powder
1 tsp (5 mL) sweet (or hot) paprika
1 tsp (5 mL) salt
1 cup (250 mL) milk
2 Tbsp (30 mL) vegetable oil (more
    if needed)
¼ cup (65 mL) sour cream
¼ cup (65 mL) Five-Spice Tomato
    Jam (page 78)
Minced chives, for garnish

In a mixing bowl, place the mashed sweet potato and eggs. Whisk to combine and then sprinkle with the flour, baking powder, paprika, and salt. Stir gently with the whisk to combine. Add the milk and gently whisk to combine into a smooth batter.

Preheat the oven to 250°F (120°C).

Heat a large non-stick skillet over medium-high heat and add a light coating of the oil. For each blini, spoon about 2 Tbsp (30 mL) of the mixture into the pan. I use a small (1 oz / 30 mL) ladle but a large spoon will also work. Make four blinis at a time, leaving about 1 inch (2.5 cm) between each one.

Fry until golden brown, crispy on the outside, and cooked through, 2 minutes per side. If the blinis start to scorch (burn), turn down the heat to medium or medium-low. Transfer to a baking sheet lined with paper towel and place in the oven to keep warm. Repeat with the remaining batter and oil. To serve, take three warm blinis and top with a dollop of sour cream and tomato jam. Scatter chives overtop and serve immediately.

STARTERS
AND
APPETIZERS

BLANCHED ASPARAGUS WITH SHALLOTS, CHILIES, AND GARLIC

Asparagus is one of those vegetables that are best the moment they're picked, full of sweetness and crunch. You can revive asparagus by cutting off the stem end and standing it in a container of water into which a little sugar has been stirred. The plant readily sucks up the liquid to re-plump the spears.

SERVES 4–6

1 lb (454 g) asparagus, trimmed

2 cups (500 mL) shredded head lettuce

1 Tbsp (15 mL) grapeseed oil

2 shallots, peeled, trimmed, and finely diced

2 small Thai chilies

1 Tbsp (15 mL) minced garlic

Salt and pepper

2 Tbsp (30 mL) chopped cilantro

In a large pot filled with salted boiling water, place the asparagus and cook for 4 to 5 minutes, or until just tender. Remove with a slotted spoon and place in a bowl filled with cold water. Drain the asparagus, cut each spear into two equal lengths, and set aside until needed.

Mound the shredded lettuce in the centre of a plate in preparation for serving.

In a large sauté pan over high heat, place the oil then the shallots. Sauté until the shallots wilt and start to brown. Add the asparagus spears and toss to coat. Add the chilies and garlic and season well with salt and pepper. Sauté until the chilies and garlic are fragrant and the asparagus is just beginning to scorch. Add the cilantro and toss to coat.

Remove the pan from the heat and tilt it to slide the asparagus mix on top of the lettuce. Serve immediately.

STUFFED TOMATOES WITH JAPANESE CUSTARD AND PICKLED PLUM

Use a meaty, thick-walled tomato for this dish. If the tomato is very round, you may have to slice off a thin sliver of skin from the bottom to allow it to sit upright on a plate. Be careful not to cut through the wall of the tomato or the filling will leak out.

SERVES 4

4 medium-size ripe tomatoes
1 Tbsp plus 1 tsp (20 mL) light
   soy sauce
1 tsp (5 mL) minced pickled ginger
1 tsp (5 mL) omiboshi
   (pickled plum paste)
1 Tbsp (15 mL) mirin
2 Tbsp (30 mL) minced shiso (perilla)
   leaf (or cilantro)
2 eggs, lightly beaten
1 cup (250 mL) Mushroom,
   Vegetable, and Miso Stock
   (page 93)
Boiling water
Sea salt flakes
Shredded nori

Preheat the oven to 325°F (160°C).

Place a tomato on a cutting board and use a small, sharp knife to remove the top. Remove the seeds and membrane with a spoon, taking care not to puncture the wall of the tomato. Place in an oven-proof container. Repeat with the remaining tomatoes.

In a mixing bowl, combine the soy sauce, pickled ginger, plum paste, and mirin. Whisk to mix and then stir in the shiso. Add the eggs and stock, whisking well to mix everything together. Pour this into a large measuring cup and fill each hollowed tomato. Pour boiling water into the baking pan, halfway up the tomatoes. Slide the pan carefully into the oven and bake for 20 minutes, or until the custard sets firmly on the outside with a little jiggle left in the centre. Remove from the oven, place on a wire rack, and allow to cool in the water. Garnish with salt flakes and some shredded nori. Served chilled or warm.

BREADED EGGPLANT AND TOMATO STACKS WITH FRESH MOZZARELLA AND GREEN OLIVE TAPENADE

This dish is a tribute to the Mediterranean with the flavors of late summer shining through. Use the best tomatoes you can find. Meaty sweet tomatoes like Brandywine or Old Flame are ideal.

SERVES 4–6

5 Tbsp (75 mL) olive oil, separated

½ cup (125 mL) pitted green olives

2 shallots, peeled, trimmed, and sliced

1 tsp (5 mL) minced garlic

1 lemon, juice and zest

1 Tbsp (15 mL) capers

1 tsp (5 mL) hot sauce

2 large eggplants

1 tsp (5 mL) sea salt

2 eggs, beaten

¼ cup (65 mL) milk

1 cup (250 mL) all-purpose flour

2 cups (500 mL) panko breadcrumbs (or dried breadcrumbs)

Grapeseed oil, for frying

4 ripe heirloom tomatoes

½ lb (about 225 g) fresh buffalo (or cow) milk mozzarella

Fresh basil leaves, for garnish

In a sauté pan over medium-high heat, place 3 Tbsp (45 mL) of the olive oil then the olives, shallots, and garlic. Sauté for 2 to 3 minutes then remove from the heat and allow to cool. Scrape the ingredients into a food processor bowl and pulse until coarsely blended. Add the lemon juice and zest, capers, and hot sauce. Pulse until smooth. Taste and adjust the flavoring with 1 tsp (5 mL) hot sauce, or to taste. Set this tapenade aside and allow to cool.

On a cutting board, trim and discard the ends of the eggplants and cut the eggplants into ½-inch (1.25 cm) slices. You should have at least 12 slices of eggplant in total at the end. Place on a roasting pan, drizzle with the remaining 2 Tbsp (30 mL) olive oil, and sprinkle with the sea salt. Let sit for 5 minutes. Preheat the broiler to hot. Place the tray under the broiler and cook the eggplant slices until the tops just begin to color. Remove from the heat and allow to cool.

Whisk the eggs with the milk in a bowl to make an egg wash. Set up a breading station with a plate of flour, the bowl of egg wash, and a plate of breadcrumbs. Season each of these with salt and pepper. Take a round of eggplant, dredge it in flour, dip in it egg wash, and dredge it in breadcrumbs. Return the eggplant slice to the tray and repeat with the remainder of the ingredients.

Heat enough grapeseed oil to shallow-fry the eggplant in a wide, shallow pot (or deep skillet) over medium heat. Add the eggplant slices in batches and cook until golden brown, turning occasionally. Transfer to a clean rimmed baking tray and keep warm.

To serve, place an eggplant round on a serving plate. Top with thin slices of tomato, slices or ripped shards of mozzarella, and a drizzle of tapenade. Top with a second round of eggplant, one more slice of tomato, and a small slice or chunk of mozzarella. Drizzle with tapenade and top with a sprig of fresh basil. Repeat with the remaining ingredients. Serve immediately.

FRITTATA WITH PURPLE POTATOES AND WARM HERB AND SOUR CREAM TOPPING

Purple potatoes are waxy and delicate potatoes. They benefit from gentle cooking as the skin tends to split if they are boiled too rapidly. They make a lovely contrast to the egg and sour cream mixture.

SERVES 4

1 lb (454 g) purple potatoes,
  scrubbed clean

4 large eggs

Salt and pepper

1 Tbsp (15 mL) olive oil

1 small onion, peeled and diced

1 Tbsp (15 mL) minced garlic

2 Tbsp (30 mL) minced fresh
  flat-leaf parsley

½ cup (125 mL) sour cream

2 green onions, trimmed and minced

In a small pot, place the clean potatoes and cover them with cold water. Bring to a boil, turn down the heat, and simmer for 10 minutes, or until the potatoes are easily pierced with a small knife. Drain and allow to cool enough to handle. Cut the potatoes into thin slices and set aside.

Preheat the broiler to high.

In a small bowl, combine the eggs with 2 Tbsp (30 mL) water. Whisk until combined and season with salt and pepper.

Heat a non-stick pan over medium-high and add the olive oil, onion, and potato slices. Cook for 5 minutes, stirring occasionally. Add the garlic and parsley. Season the onion and potatoes with salt and pepper and add the egg mixture to the pan. Turn down the heat to low. When the eggs begin to set, take a spatula and gently push the egg away from the side of the pan. Tilt the pan to allow any uncooked egg in the centre to flow to the edges. Swirl the pan to allow the egg to cover the bottom of the pan.

In a small bowl, mix the sour cream with the green onions. Season with salt and pepper. Spread over the egg and potato mixture. Place under the broiler and cook until the sour cream begins to brown and bubble. Remove from the heat and allow to sit for 1 to 2 minutes. Cut into wedges and serve warm.

POTATO CROQUETTES WITH MUSHROOMS, TRUFFLES, AND BLUE CHEESE CREAM

Russet potatoes make the best mashed potatoes and croquettes because the starch content makes the mash fluffy and light. To make 3 cups (750 mL) of mashed potato you will need about 1.5 lb (680 g) of raw, peeled russet potatoes.

SERVES 4–6

3 eggs

3 cups (750 mL) cooked
    mashed potato

¼ cup (65 mL) grated
    Parmesan cheese

Salt and pepper

All-purpose flour, for dusting

1 Tbsp (15 mL) butter

1 Tbsp (15 mL) minced garlic

2 cups (500 mL) diced mushrooms
    (button, chanterelle, oyster, etc.)

1 tsp (5 mL) truffle paste (or good
    truffle oil)

1 cup (250 mL) all-purpose flour

¼ cup (65 mL) milk

2 cups (500 mL) panko breadcrumbs
    (or dried breadcrumbs)

½ cup (125 mL) grapeseed oil

1 cup (250 mL) whipping cream

¼ cup (65 mL) crumbled blue cheese

Minced chives, for garnish

Beat one of the eggs. In a mixing bowl, combine the mashed potato, Parmesan cheese, and beaten egg. Season with salt and pepper and mix until well blended. Turn the potato onto a floured work surface and knead it into a solid mass. Sprinkle with flour and form several large tubes about 1 inch (2.5 cm) in thickness. Set aside while you make the filling.

In a sauté pan over medium-high heat, place the butter and heat it until sizzling. Add the garlic then the mushrooms and heat to release and evaporate the liquid. Stir in the truffle paste and season well with salt and pepper. Remove from the heat and allow to cool slightly.

On a well-floured work surface, take a section of potato rope and flatten it slightly with your hands. Use a chopstick to push a groove into the centre of the length of potato. Fill with a little of the mushroom mixture. Fold the two sides together to envelop the filling and gently roll into a cylinder. Cut into 2-inch (5 cm) logs and set them on a tray. Repeat with the remaining potato and filling. You should end up with 12 to 15 pieces. Place the tray in the fridge to chill for at least 1 hour.

Preheat the oven to 350°F (180°C).

Whisk the remaining two eggs with the milk in a bowl to make an egg wash. Set up a breading station with a plate of flour, the bowl of egg wash, and a plate of breadcrumbs. Season each one with salt and pepper. Take a cylinder of potato, roll it in flour, dip it in egg wash, and then roll it in the breadcrumbs. Return to the tray and repeat with the remaining ingredients. Chill for at least 30 minutes.

Heat enough grapeseed oil to shallow-fry the croquettes in a wide shallow pot (or deep skillet) over medium heat. Add the croquettes in batches and cook until golden brown, turning occasionally. Transfer to a clean baking tray and keep warm in the oven while you make the sauce.

In a saucepan, place the cream and bring it to a boil. Turn off the heat immediately and add the cheese. Season with black pepper and cool until the cheese melts and the sauce thickens slightly.

Spoon a little sauce on each plate and top with three croquettes. Garnish with fresh chives and serve immediately.

CIDER-BRAISED LEEK AND MOREL GRATIN

The French perfected the art of the gratin with many savory and sweet applications. This dish would be at home in any of the northern countryside areas of the France. Use large leeks that have a nice long section of white stem. The mild flavor pairs well with the cream, and the morels add an earthy tone and will absorb all the richness of the sauce. Do not allow the sauce to boil after the egg yolks have been added—it will split.

SERVES 4–6

1 cup (250 mL) dried morels
4 large leeks, trimmed, split,
   and washed
2 Tbsp (30 mL) butter
1 Tbsp (15 mL) minced garlic
1 cup (250 mL) dry apple cider
1 cup (250 mL) whipping cream
1 Tbsp (15 mL) minced thyme leaves
2 egg yolks
Additional cream to thin yolks
Salt and pepper

In a heatproof bowl, place the morels and cover them with boiling water. Drain immediately in a sieve and return to the bowl. Cover again with boiling water and allow to sit for 15 minutes or until the water cools.

On a cutting board, trim off most of the deep green sections of the leek. Cut the stem into 3-inch (7.5 cm) chunks and split the halves lengthwise in two (split them again if the leeks are really large). Place the leeks in a sauté pan and add the butter and garlic. Gently sauté the leeks over medium heat for 1 to 2 minutes. Drain the morels, cut them into rings, and add them to the leeks. Add the apple cider. Bring to a boil, turn down the heat, and simmer until the leeks are soft, about 15 minutes. Add the cream and thyme and cook until the mixture thickens and coats the back of a spoon, about 5 minutes.

Heat the broiler to hot.

In a small bowl, whisk the egg yolks with a little cream. Remove the leeks from the heat and stir the yolks into the warm sauce. Season with salt and pepper to taste. Transfer to a gratin dish. Place under the hot boiler and heat until the top browns and bubbles. Remove from the heat and let cool slightly before serving with crispy French bread.

CAULIFLOWER, SESAME, AND CURRIED MUSHROOM PAKORA WITH GINGER-LIME SAUCE

This pakora recipe works with a wide variety of vegetables. Try broccoli, green beans, green onions, and cooked squash for tasty results. You can also vary the spice mix by using the Spanish Seasoning Powder (page 85) or Five-Spice Powder (page 81).

SERVES 4–6

1 head cauliflower

2 cups (500 mL) chickpea flour

2 Tbsp (30 mL) toasted sesame seeds

1 Tbsp (15 mL) Mushroom Curry Powder (page 82)

1 tsp (5 mL) salt

2 green onions, trimmed and minced

1 tsp (5 mL) minced garlic

1½ cups (375 mL) water

2 Tbsp (30 mL) ginger (or orange) marmalade

1 lime, juice and zest

2 cups (500 mL) grapeseed oil

On a cutting board, trim and cut the cauliflower into bite-size chunks. Heat a pot of water to boiling and add the cauliflower. Turn down the heat and simmer until just tender, 4 to 5 minutes. Drain and set aside to cool.

In a mixing bowl, combine the chickpea flour, sesame seeds, Mushroom Curry Powder, salt, green onions, and garlic. Add just enough water to make the batter come together like a thick pancake batter. Start with 1 cup (250 mL) and add the rest slowly, to achieve a smooth batter. In a small bowl, combine the marmalade and lime juice and zest.

Preheat the oven to 350°F (180°C).

In a large, thick-bottomed pot, bring the grapeseed oil to a temperature of 375°F (190°C). Test the temperature by dropping in a bit of batter. It should bubble vigorously and immediately float to the surface. Dip the cauliflower chunks into the batter and add to the hot oil in batches. Do not crowd the pan. Remove the cauliflower with a slotted spoon when golden brown and place on a tray covered with paper towels. Transfer to the oven to keep warm while you cook the remaining cauliflower.

To serve, transfer to a serving platter and drizzle with the ginger-lime sauce.

MIXED
SALADS

CRISPY BREAD SALAD WITH ROASTED CHANTERELLES AND BRUSSELS SPROUTS

This is a great tapas-style salad that works well as an appetizer with a glass of wine or as a side dish for a festive dinner with company. The salad is best eaten soon after it is mixed with the dressing. It will still taste great the next day, but the subtle crunch of the bread will be absent.

SERVES 4

1 lb (454 g) Brussels sprouts, trimmed

½ lb (225 g) chanterelle (or oyster) mushrooms

2 Tbsp (30 mL) olive oil

1 Tbsp (15 mL) Spanish Seasoning Powder (page 85)

Salt and pepper

2 Tbsp (30 mL) grapeseed oil

2 Tbsp (30 mL) butter

1 Tbsp (15 mL) minced garlic

4 cups (1 L) cubed bread (rustic white loaf, baguette, etc.)

2 Tbsp (30 mL) grated Parmesan cheese

1 Tbsp (15 mL) orange marmalade

1 lemon, juice and zest

2 Tbsp (30 mL) olive oil

2 Tbsp (30 mL) chopped fresh flat-leaf parsley

Preheat the oven to 350°F (180°C).

On a rimmed baking tray, combine the Brussels sprouts, mushrooms, olive oil, and spice powder. Toss to coat and season well with salt and pepper. Place in the oven and roast for about 20 minutes, or until the Brussels sprouts are soft and browned. Remove from the oven and let cool to room temperature.

In a sauté pan over medium-high heat, place the grapeseed oil, butter, and garlic. When sizzling, add the bread cubes and sauté for 3 to 4 minutes, or until they absorb the seasoning and just begin to brown. Add the cheese and toss quickly to evenly cover the bread cubes. Transfer to a platter lined with paper towels and allow to cool.

In a small bowl, combine the marmalade and lemon juice and zest. Whisk to combine. Add the olive oil in a slow and steady stream, whisking until it is incorporated and smooth.

In a mixing bowl, combine the roasted Brussels sprouts and mushrooms with the bread cubes. Drizzle half the dressing overtop and toss to mix. Transfer to a serving plate or platter and drizzle a little of the remaining dressing around it. Garnish with the parsley and serve at room temperature.

WILD RICE SALAD WITH SWEET PEPPERS, APPLES, CUCUMBER, AND FETA

This dish has all the appeal of a great salad with the nutty flavor of wild rice adding interest and texture. This can of salad can be readily adapted to your personal taste. You can add a couple of cloves of garlic to the rice water to infuse the grains with flavor. Add fresh tomatoes as a garnish. Or add any other vegetable you would put into a chopped salad—green beans, broccoli, and cauliflower would fit well into the mix. Use your favorite apple—Fuji and Gala are nice choices. Use ⅔ cup (150 mL) wild rice to make 2 cups (500 mL) cooked rice.

SERVES 4–6

2 Tbsp (30 mL) sherry (or red wine)
  vinegar
1 Tbsp (15 mL) prepared
  grainy mustard
1 tsp (5 mL) hot sauce
1 Tbsp (15 mL) minced fresh oregano
  or flat-leaf parsley
3 Tbsp (45 mL) olive oil
2 cups (500 mL) cooked wild rice,
  cooled
1 red bell pepper, seeded and
  finely diced
1 yellow bell pepper, seeded and
  finely diced
1 cup (250 mL) diced English
  cucumber
1 large apple, skin on,
  cored and diced
Salt and pepper
½ cup (125 mL) crumbled feta cheese
Toasted sunflower seeds

In a small mixing bowl, whisk together the vinegar, mustard, hot sauce, and herbs with 1 tablespoon (15 mL) water. Drizzle in the oil in a steady stream, whisking until incorporated and thick.

In a mixing bowl, combine the wild rice, bell peppers, cucumber, and apple. Add half the dressing and toss well to coat. Taste, and season with salt and pepper if necessary. Transfer to a serving plate and top with the crumbled feta and sunflower seeds. Drizzle the remaining dressing around the salad. Serve at room temperature.

BARLEY SALAD WITH GREENS AND SWEET AND SOUR TOMATO DRESSING

This is an excellent use of the Five-Spice Tomato Jam recipe (page 78). If you don't have any, you can soak a handful of sundried tomatoes, drain them, and purée them with 1 tablespoon (15 mL) honey and ½ teaspoon (2.5 mL) of Five-Spice Powder (page 81). This is also a great dish for the wintertime if you use local hothouse tomatoes. Use ½ cup (125 mL) barley, cooked with 2 cups (500 mL) water, to yield about 2 cups (500 mL) of drained, cooked barley.

SERVES 4–6

1 lime, juice and zest

2 Tbsp (30 mL) Five-Spice Tomato Jam (page 78)

1 tsp (5 mL) hot sauce

3 Tbsp (45 mL) olive oil

2 cups (500 mL) cooked barley, cooled

2 cups (500 mL) chopped greens (arugula, mizuna, baby kale, spinach, etc.)

4 medium tomatoes, cored and diced

1 cup (250 mL) diced English cucumber

Salt and pepper

Toasted sesame seeds

In a mixing bowl, whisk together the lime juice and zest, tomato jam, and hot sauce. Drizzle in the oil in a steady stream, whisking until incorporated and thick.

In a mixing bowl, combine the barley, chopped greens, tomatoes, and cucumber. Add half the dressing and toss well to coat. Taste, and then season with salt and pepper if needed. Transfer to a serving plate and top with the sesame seeds. Drizzle the remaining dressing around the salad. Serve immediately.

SPROUTS, MICRO GREENS, CARROT, AND CRISPY RICE NOODLE SALAD

You can fry your own rice noodles to create puffy and crispy noodles. You can also buy fried chow mein noodles in many grocery stores. If you heat them quickly in a hot oven and then let them cool, this will refresh the flavor and make a great addition to the salad. If micro greens are not available, use a variety of sprouts like sunflower, bean sprouts, and alfalfa.

SERVES 4–6

2 cups (500 mL) grapeseed oil (for frying)

2 oz (60 g) dry, thin rice noodles

1 tsp (5 mL) Mushroom Curry Powder (page 82) (or Five-Spice Powder, page 81)

Salt and pepper

1 Tbsp (15 mL) prepared mustard

2 Tbsp (30 mL) rice vinegar

1 Tbsp (15 mL) light soy sauce

1 tsp (5 mL) sesame oil

1 Tbsp (15 mL) minced cilantro

1 tsp (5 mL) minced garlic

3 Tbsp (45 mL) grapeseed oil

2 cups (500 mL) micro greens (or young salad mix)

1 cup (250 mL) sunflower or mung bean sprouts

1 cup (250 mL) shredded carrot

Cilantro leaves, for garnish

Sesame seeds, for garnish

Heat the grapeseed oil in a wide, deep pot over medium heat to 375°F (190°C). Test the temperature by dropping a strand of noodle into the oil. It should bubble and expand quickly. Break up the dried noodles with your hands and add a little at a time to the oil. They will steam and bubble vigorously. Be careful to use a pot with deep enough sides to contain this action. Fry until the noodles are puffy but still pure white. Transfer to a tray lined witn paper towels to absorb any excess oil. Repeat with the remaining rice noodles. Season with the curry powder, salt, and pepper and set aside.

In a small bowl, whisk together the mustard with the rice vinegar, soy sauce, sesame oil, cilantro, and garlic. Add the grapeseed oil in a slow, steady stream, whisking until smooth and thick.

In a salad bowl, combine the micro greens, bean sprouts, and carrot. Drizzle with half the dressing and toss well to coat. Add the fried noodles and toss to coat. Taste, and then season with salt and pepper if needed. Garnish with the cilantro leaves and toasted sesame seeds. Serve immediately.

SUI CHOY, CUCUMBER, AND ROSE PETAL KIMCHI

The rose petals add a mysterious flavor and wonderful color to the salad. Only use organic rose petals, as fresh as possible, for this dish. Florists' roses may be sprayed with pesticides or treated with preservatives. This is a fresh kimchi that can be made and eaten the same day. If left to ferment (for up to a week), it will develop a more complex, salty flavor with acidity added to the mix. You can substitute green or savoy cabbage with excellent results.

SERVES 4–6

1 sui choy (napa) cabbage, washed

1 English cucumber, thinly sliced

1 cup (250 mL) rose petals, washed

6 green onions, trimmed and chopped

2 Tbsp (30 mL) minced garlic

2 Tbsp (30 mL) minced ginger

1 Tbsp (15 mL) minced fresh hot pepper (or 1 tsp/5 mL ground cayenne)

1 Tbsp (15 mL) brown sugar

1 Tbsp (15 mL) salt

2 Tbsp (30 mL) light soy sauce

1 tsp (5 mL) sesame oil

Toasted sesame seeds, for garnish

On a cutting board, place the sui choy and split it in half. Remove the solid core at the base. Shred the cabbage into strips.

In a glass mixing or salad bowl, combine the sui choy, cucumber, rose petals, green onions, garlic, ginger, hot pepper, brown sugar, salt, soy sauce, and sesame oil. Toss well to coat. Leave on the counter for about 1 hour, tossing occasionally.

To serve, remove the ingredients from the liquid and drain or squeeze gently to remove any excess moisture. Transfer to a serving plate and sprinkle with toasted sesame seeds before serving.

LEEK AND MUSHROOM KIMCHI

In Korea, kimchi is made with a number of seasonings and spices. This version uses lightly cooked leeks and mushrooms brightly seasoned with garlic, ginger, and chilies. It will keep for about 1 week in the fridge and is great as an accompaniment to any of the vegetable, potato, or sweet potato pancakes in this book.

SERVES 4–6

4 large leeks, split and washed

1 Tbsp (15 mL) grapeseed oil

2 cups (500 mL) sliced mushrooms
   (button, shiitake, oyster,
   chanterelles, etc.)

1 Tbsp (15 mL) minced garlic

1 Tbsp (15 mL) minced ginger

1 Tbsp (15 mL) minced fresh hot
   pepper (or 1 tsp/5 mL
   ground cayenne)

2 Tbsp (30 mL) miso paste

2 Tbsp (30 mL) sweet white wine
   vinegar (or half mirin and half
   rice vinegar)

1 Tbsp (15 mL) light soy sauce

1 tsp (5 mL) sesame oil

Salt and pepper

Toasted sesame seeds, for garnish

On a cutting board, trim any dark green tips from the leeks, leaving only the light green and white parts. Remove any hard core from the leeks then them cut into 1-inch (2.5 cm) slices. Cover with cold water and set aside until needed.

Heat the grapeseed oil in a sauté pan over medium-high heat, then add the mushrooms. Add the garlic, ginger, hot pepper, and miso paste. Sauté until the mushrooms release their moisture and the pan cooks dry. Drain the leeks and add them to the pan, tossing it to warm through and just wilt them.

Transfer the mixture to a glass mixing or salad bowl and add the vinegar, soy sauce, and sesame oil. Season well with salt and pepper to taste.

Allow to cool to room temperature and garnish with toasted sesame seeds before serving.

FENNEL SALAD WITH ESPRESSO VINAIGRETTE AND GOAT CHEESE

The dressing is made with fresh espresso. You can also make strong coffee with a French press with good results. Reducing espresso tends to create a bitter flavor, and adding a little maple syrup or honey helps counter this and creates a sweet base to help balance the dressing.

SERVES 4–6

¼ cup (65 mL) fresh espresso

1 tsp (5 mL) maple syrup or honey

1 Tbsp (15 mL) white wine vinegar

1 orange, juice and zest

4 Tbsp (60 mL) grapeseed oil

2 bulbs fennel, stalks removed

1 red onion, peeled and trimmed

1 Tbsp (15 mL) Spanish Seasoning
    Powder (page 85)

Salt and pepper

¼ cup (65 mL) crumbled goat cheese

In a saucepan, combine the espresso and maple syrup. Bring to a boil and reduce to about half the volume. Set aside to cool.

In a mixing bowl, whisk together the reduced coffee syrup, vinegar, and orange juice and zest. Drizzle in the oil in a steady stream, whisking until incorporated and thick.

On a cutting board, trim off any dark green tips of the fennel bulb, leaving only the light green and white parts. If the outer leaves are bruised or dry, remove them. Cut the fennel in half lengthwise and remove any solid, hard core at the base of the bulb. With a sharp knife or mandolin, shred the fennel as thinly as possible then place it in a salad bowl. Cut the red onion as thinly as possible and add it to the fennel.

Season with the spice powder, salt, and pepper, and toss well to coat. Let sit for at least 30 minutes. Just before serving, toss with half the dressing and mix well. Transfer to a serving plate, top with the crumbled goat cheese, and drizzle a little of the excess dressing around the plate. Serve at room temperature.

HEIRLOOM POTATO AND SMOKED EGG SALAD

This salad looks best when you use a vibrant mix of potatoes. You can find white, yellow, red, pink, and blue potatoes. If you use small nugget varieties, you can wash them and use them whole. If you don't have a smoker, you can use smoked Spanish paprika in the salad to give you similar flavors.

SERVES 4–6

4 eggs, room temperature

1 Tbsp (15 mL) brown sugar

1 Tbsp (15 mL) soy sauce

1 Tbsp (15 mL) hot sauce

Salt and pepper

2 lb (about 900 g) mixed potatoes, scrubbed clean

4 green onions, trimmed and minced

2 Tbsp (30 mL) mayonnaise

2 Tbsp (30 mL) sour cream

1 Tbsp (15 mL) white wine vinegar

1 tsp (5 mL) honey

Chives, for garnish

Sweet (or smoked) paprika, for garnish

Preheat the smoker to 150°F (65°C).

In a saucepan, bring 4 cups (1 L) of water to a boil, turn down the heat to a simmer, and gently add the eggs using a large spoon. Cook for 4 minutes, then remove them from the heat and drain. Run the eggs under cold water until they are cool enough to handle. Peel them and place them in a small bowl. Add the sugar, soy sauce, and hot sauce. Season with salt and pepper and toss well to mix. Let sit for 15 minutes, turning occasionally.

Remove the eggs from the marinade, set the marinade aside, and place the eggs on a wire rack. Place them in the smoker and infuse with smoke for about 30 minutes. Remove the eggs from the smoker and place them back in the marinade. This can be done up to 1 day in advance.

In a large pot, cover the potatoes with cold water. Bring to a boil, turn down the heat, and simmer until the potatoes are easily pierced with a fork, about 10 minutes. Drain and allow to cool slightly.

In a mixing bowl, combine the mayonnaise, sour cream, vinegar, and honey. Season with salt and pepper. On a cutting board, cut the potatoes into slices or quarters (they should be bite-size) and add to the dressing. Remove the eggs from the marinade and cut them into slices or wedges. Add to the potatoes and toss well to coat.

Transfer everything to a serving plate and garnish with a sprinkling of chives and paprika. Serve at room temperature.

CASSEROLES AND BRAISES

MUSHROOM AND VEGETABLE SHEPHERD'S PIE

This is classic comfort food for a cold winter's night. If you have preserved or frozen some tomatoes from the garden, this is a good way to use them. If you use canned tomatoes, look for low-salt varieties. For a little more richness, you can fold fresh goat cheese into the potatoes, or sprinkle a little on top before you bake the dish.

SERVES 6–8

2 lb (about 1 kg) russet
   potatoes, scrubbed
¼ cup (65 mL) sour cream
2 Tbsp (30 mL) butter
Salt and pepper
1 Tbsp (15 mL) olive oil
1 cup (250 mL) chopped onion
2 cups (500 mL) sliced mushrooms
   (button, oyster, chanterelle, etc.)
1 Tbsp (15 mL) minced garlic
1 cup (250 mL) diced carrot
1 cup (250 mL) diced celery
1 cup (250 mL) chopped broccoli
4 cups (1 L) stewed tomatoes
1 Tbsp (15 mL) minced
   fresh rosemary
1 Tbsp (15 mL) minced fresh sage

In a large saucepan, cover the potatoes with lightly salted cold water. Bring to a boil, turn down the heat to medium, and cook for 20 minutes, or until all the potatoes are easily pierced with a knife.

Drain the potatoes and let them cool enough to handle and peel. While they are still warm, mash the potatoes with a ricer, food mill, or masher. Return them to the saucepan (if necessary) and add the sour cream and butter. Stir well to mix until smooth and creamy and season well with salt and pepper. Keep warm.

In a large pot over medium-high heat, place the olive oil, onion, mushrooms, and garlic. Sauté until the mushrooms release their moisture and add the carrot, celery, and broccoli. Sauté, stirring, until the vegetables are warmed through and just begin to brown. Add the tomatoes, rosemary, and sage. Bring to a boil, turn down the heat to a simmer, and cook for 1 hour, or until the tomatoes start to break down and the sauce thickens. Taste, and season with salt and pepper if necessary.

Preheat the oven to 350°F (180°C).

Transfer the vegetables to a casserole dish (13- × 9-inch / 33 × 23 cm) and spread them evenly across the bottom. Scoop spoonfuls of mashed potatoes overtop and gently spread it across the surface. Place the casserole in the oven and bake until the potato begins to brown, about 30 minutes. Serve hot.

BAKED RICE WITH CORN AND SPICED BÉCHAMEL

This is a rich and comforting dish that would be welcome on a cool night. You can use leftover steamed rice or make a fresh batch of short-grain rice. Roughly 1½ cups (375 mL) of rice cooked with 3 cups (750 mL) of water will yield about 4 cups (1 L) of cooked rice.

SERVES 6–8

2 Tbsp (30 mL) butter

2 Tbsp (30 mL) all-purpose flour

2 cups (500 mL) milk

1 cup (250 mL) shredded
    mozzarella cheese

1 Tbsp (15 mL) Spanish Seasoning
    Powder (page 85)

4 cups (1 L) cooked short-grain rice
    (white or brown)

2 cups (500 mL) cooked
    (or frozen) corn

1 cup (250 mL) chopped greens (kale,
    spinach, mustards, etc.)

Preheat the oven to 350°F (180°C).

In a saucepan over medium heat, melt the butter. Toss in the flour and whisk to incorporate. Add ½ cup (125 mL) of the milk and quickly mix to dissolve any lumps and leave a smooth paste. The paste will thicken as it cooks. Add ¾ cup (180 mL) more milk and whisk until smooth. Add the remaining milk and whisk to blend. Turn down the heat and simmer, stirring occasionally, until the mixture thickens, about 5 minutes. Add the mozzarella cheese and spice powder. Stir to melt the cheese. Remove from the heat and set aside until needed.

In a casserole dish (13- × 9-inch / 33 × 23 cm), mix together the rice, corn, and greens, breaking up any lumps of rice. Spread the béchamel sauce evenly overtop. Place in the oven and bake until the top is browned and bubbling, about 30 minutes. Serve hot.

EGGPLANT WITH PORCINI BÉCHAMEL

Porcini powder adds a caramel and mushroom note to the sauce. This casserole is delicious when eaten hot out of the oven or left for a day and reheated. You can use large purple eggplants, or about twice as many smaller Japanese eggplants. Cut these on an angle to get a bigger surface area.

SERVES 6–8

2 Tbsp (30 mL) butter

2 Tbsp (30 mL) all-purpose flour

2 cups (500 mL) milk

1 Tbsp (15 mL) ground dried
    porcini mushrooms

1 Tbsp (15 mL) minced garlic

1 Tbsp (15 mL) minced
    fresh rosemary

1 cup (250 mL) shredded
    mozzarella cheese

Salt and pepper

3 large eggplants

Olive oil

Preheat the oven to 350°F (180°C).

In a saucepan over medium heat, melt the butter. Toss in the flour and whisk to incorporate. Add ½ cup (125 mL) of the milk and quickly mix it to dissolve any lumps and leave a smooth paste. The paste will thicken as it cooks. Add another ¾ cup (180 mL) of the milk and whisk until smooth. Add the remaining milk with the dried mushrooms, garlic, and rosemary. Whisk to blend. Turn down the heat and simmer, stirring occasionally, until the mixture thickens, about 5 minutes. Add the mozzarella cheese and stir to melt the cheese and form a smooth sauce. Taste, and then season well with salt and pepper. Remove from the heat and set aside until needed.

On a cutting board, trim off and discard the ends of the eggplant and cut the eggplant into ½-inch (1.25 cm) slices. Place them on a roasting pan, sprinkle with sea salt and olive oil, and let sit for 5 minutes.

Preheat the broiler to hot. Place the tray under the broiler and cook the eggplant until the top just begins to color. Remove from the heat and allow to cool.

In an oiled casserole dish (13- × 9-inch / 33 × 23 cm), place a layer of eggplant, top with a thin layer of the béchamel, and repeat with the remaining ingredients, ending with an even layer of béchamel. Place in the oven and bake until the top is browned and bubbling, about 30 minutes. Serve hot.

SAVOY CABBAGE ROLLS WITH MUSHROOMS, HERBS, AND RICE

This dish is a spin on the traditional cabbage roll and features the flavors of French onion soup. You could add a little sherry to the stock for a nice effect. If the spine is really dominant on the cabbage leaves, you can trim it off before preparing the recipe. Roughly 1½ cups (375 mL) rice cooked with 3 cups (750 mL) of water will yield about 4 cups (1 L) of cooked rice.

SERVES 6–8

1 head savoy cabbage

1 tsp (5 mL) salt

4 cups (1 L) cooked short-grain rice (white or brown)

2 cups (500 mL) diced mushrooms (button, shiitake, oyster, morel, etc.)

1 cup (250 mL) chopped spinach (or kale, mustard greens, etc.)

Salt and pepper

2 cups (500 mL) Caramelized Onion and Mushroom Stock (page 91)

1 cup (250 mL) aged strong cheese (Gouda, Gruyère, Manchego, cheddar, etc.)

Preheat the oven to 350°F (180°C).

On a cutting board, cut the bottom off the cabbage and use a small sharp knife to remove the hard core. Gently peel off the leaves, leaving them as whole as possible.

Bring a large stockpot of water to a boil. Add the salt and as many cabbage leaves as fit comfortably in the pot. Stir gently with a slotted spoon until the leaves become pliable, 3 to 4 minutes. Remove from the pot with a slotted spoon and transfer to a bowl of cold water. When cool, transfer to a tray. Repeat with the remaining cabbage leaves.

In a mixing bowl, combine the cooked rice, diced mushrooms, and spinach. Season well with salt and pepper. Lay a cabbage leaf on a cutting board and place a spoonful of rice on the stem end of the leaf. Fold over to make a tight cylinder. Fold in the edges and roll toward the edge of the leaf. Place the roll, seam side down, in a casserole dish large enough to hold all the cabbage rolls. Repeat with the remaining leaves and filling. Heat the stock and pour it over the cabbage rolls. Sprinkle the cheese overtop.

Place in the oven and bake until the cheese is browned and bubbling, about 30 minutes. Serve hot.

RED CABBAGE BRAISED WITH APPLE AND MISO

The humble red cabbage transforms into something truly delicious in this recipe. The apples bring sweetness to the finish and the miso adds umami and nuttiness. Caraway seed is a personal favorite of mine with cabbage, but you could add fennel seed or grainy mustard to the mix. Use your favorite type of apple. Fuji and Gala are two nice choices.

SERVES 4–6

1 head red cabbage

2 apples, peeled

1 onion, peeled and thinly sliced

1 cup (250 mL) apple cider

1 cup (250 mL) Aromatic Vegetable
    Stock (page 90) (or water)

2 Tbsp (30 mL) apple cider vinegar

2 Tbsp (30 mL) miso paste

1 Tbsp (15 mL) caraway seed

1 Tbsp (15 mL) minced ginger

¼ cup (65 mL) toasted walnuts

Salt and pepper

On a cutting board, cut the bottom off the cabbage and cut the head in half. Cut it into quarters and remove the hard core at the centre. Using a sharp knife, shred the cabbage thinly. Place the cabbage in a large stainless steel saucepan. Grate the apples and add them to the cabbage.

Place the saucepan over medium-high heat and add the onion, cider, stock, vinegar, miso paste, caraway seed, and ginger. Stir well to blend. Bring to a boil, turn down the heat, and simmer until the cabbage is tender, about 30 minutes. Stir occasionally. Taste, and season with salt and pepper if necessary. Garnish with walnuts and serve warm or at room temperature.

GARLIC SCAPES WITH SAKE, MISO, AND GINGER

This is a delicious and slightly decadent dish that tastes of Japan. Spoon the gratin over sushi rice for a wonderful main meal or appetizer. Use more wasabi if you like. If you can find fresh wasabi root, this is a good dish for using its delicate flavors. Garlic scapes are removed from the garlic plant to stop its growth and put more resources into creating plump garlic bulbs. They are usually available in the middle of summer.

SERVES 4–6

1 lb (454 g) garlic scapes

1 tsp (5 mL) salt

1 Tbsp (15 mL) minced
    pickled ginger

½ cup (125 mL) mayonnaise

¼ cup (65 mL) sake

2 Tbsp (30 mL) mirin

2 Tbsp (30 mL) miso paste

2 tsp (10 mL) wasabi paste

1 tsp (5 mL) sesame oil

Toasted sesame seeds, for garnish

Wash the garlic scapes and snap off the bottoms of the stems. They will naturally break where the stalk is tender. Cut the scapes into 2-inch (5 cm) chunks and set aside. Bring a stockpot of water to a boil over high heat. Add the scapes and salt. Cook for 5 to 6 minutes, or until the scapes are just tender. Set aside and keep warm.

In a small bowl, combine the ginger with the mayonnaise, sake, mirin, miso, wasabi, and sesame oil. Whisk to blend smoothly.

Preheat the broiler to high.

Place the drained scapes in an oiled casserole dish (13- × 9-inch / 33 × 23 cm). Add the sauce and spread evenly overtop of the garlic scapes. Place under the broiler and cook until the sauce bubbles and begins to slightly char, about 3–4 minutes. Remove from the oven and allow to cool slightly before serving. Garnish with sesame seeds and serve over warm short-grain or sushi rice.

BRAISED FENNEL WITH APPLE CIDER, SAGE, AND GARLIC

Use a dry English-style cider for this recipe. The flavor will penetrate the fennel and turn it into a tender and juicy treat. The dish can be made in advance and reheated before serving. You can serve it as a brothy sauce or you can strain the vegetables, reduce the sauce by half, and add 1 tablespoon (15 mL) of butter. Remove the sauce from the heat and swirl to dissolve the butter. Return the fennel to the pan and toss to warm through.

SERVES 4–6

3 bulbs fennel, trimmed

1 onion, peeled and thinly sliced

1 cup (250 mL) apple cider

1 cup (250 mL) Aromatic Vegetable
　　Stock (page 90) (or water)

2 Tbsp (30 mL) minced sage leaves

1 Tbsp (15 mL) minced garlic

Toasted hazelnuts, for garnish

On a cutting board, trim off any green tips from the fennel bulbs, leaving only the light green and white parts. Cut each bulb into quarters and shave off a little of the solid core, leaving enough behind to keep the leaves together.

In a sauté pan, place the fennel, onion, apple cider, stock, sage, and garlic. Bring to a boil over high heat, then turn down the heat to a simmer. Cook, covered, for 15 to 20 minutes, or until the fennel is very tender.

Transfer to a serving dish and garnish with toasted hazelnuts. Serve immediately.

FENNEL BREAD PUDDING

Savory bread pudding is comforting and hearty fare for the fall and winter seasons. It is great when fresh and excellent reheated the next day as part of a lunch with a side of salad. You can vary the vegetables in the mix. Peppers, leeks, squash, broccoli, and cauliflower would all work.

SERVES 4–6

3 bulbs fennel, trimmed
2 Tbsp (30 mL) butter
1 cup (250 mL) finely diced onion
1 cup (250 mL) finely diced celery
1 cup (250 mL) finely diced carrot
4 cups (1 L) light cream
6 eggs
1 Tbsp (15 mL) minced sage leaves
1 Tbsp (15 mL) minced garlic
Salt and pepper
1 baguette, cut in thin slices
1 cup (250 mL) shredded
    mozzarella cheese

Preheat the oven to 325°F (160°C).

On a cutting board, trim any dark green tips from the fennel bulb, leaving only the light green and white parts. Cut each bulb into quarters, shave off a little of the solid core, and then cut into dice.

In a sauté pan over medium-high heat, place the butter, then the fennel, onion, celery, and carrot. Sauté until the vegetables begin to brown, 6 to 7 minutes. Remove from the heat and set aside until needed.

In a mixing bowl, whisk the cream with the eggs then add the sage and garlic. Season with salt and pepper and allow the mixture to settle.

Place a spoonful of the cream mixture on the bottom of an oiled casserole dish (13- × 9-inch / 33 × 23 cm) and cover it with a layer of baguette slices. Top with a sprinkling of the fennel mixture and top with another layer of bread. Ladle more of the mixture on top and repeat with the remaining bread and ingredients, ending with a layer of liquid. Press down with a spatula to saturate all the bread. Top with the cheese and place it in the oven. Bake for about 40 minutes, until the pudding is set and the top is golden and slightly puffed. Remove from the heat and allow to cool slightly before serving.

GRATIN OF CELERIAC, POTATO, AND TRUFFLE

This dish benefits from being made the day before and refrigerated overnight. Cut it into portions and place them on a parchment-covered tray to reheat in a hot oven. Use the best truffles you can find. I highly recommend using white or black truffle paste if possible. White truffle paste is the most expensive and strongly scented with a garlic edge. Black truffle paste is refined and earthy. Either will work as a great substitute for real truffles, which are pricey and hard to source in peak condition. Use truffle oil that has truffle listed as one of the ingredients. If it says truffle aroma, it is likely an artificial flavor.

SERVES 4–6

4 cups (1 L) milk

1 Tbsp (15 mL) minced sage leaves

1 Tbsp (15 mL) minced
    rosemary leaves

1 Tbsp (15 mL) minced garlic

1 bay leaf

1 tsp (5 mL) black or white truffle
    paste (or shavings of real truffle
    to taste)

Salt and pepper

1 tsp (5 mL) black or white truffle oil
    (or to taste)

1 large celeriac bulb, washed

2 large russet potatoes, peeled

1 cup (250 mL) grated aged white
    cheddar cheese

Preheat the oven to 350°F (180°C).

In a large saucepan, place the milk, sage, rosemary, garlic, bay leaf, and truffle paste. Season very well with salt and pepper and bring to a boil over high heat. Remove from the heat immediately (or the cream will foam violently when boiled) and set aside to infuse and cool slightly. After about 15 minutes, strain the mixture and stir in the truffle oil to taste.

Place the celeriac on a cutting board and cut off each end. Turn the bulb on its end and cut off the rough flesh with a sharp knife. Peel down until you reach a smooth white surface. Rinse and transfer to a clean cutting board. Using a mandolin, cut the celeriac and potatoes into very thin slices, then place them in a bowl and set aside until needed.

In an oiled casserole dish (13- × 9-inch / 33 × 23 cm), pour a ladleful of the milk mixture into the bottom of the dish. Add a layer of potato, followed by a layer of celeriac. Top with another ladle of milk and repeat with the remaining ingredients, ending with a layer of milk. Press down with a spatula.

Sprinkle with the cheese and place in the oven. Bake until a knife will easily penetrate the layers and the top is golden and bubbly, about 40 minutes. If the casserole appears to be browning too quickly, turn the oven down to 325°F (160°C). When the vegetables are cooked through, remove from the oven and allow to cool slightly. Serve warm.

ROASTED
AND
STUFFED

SALT-ROASTED CARROTS WITH CHINESE SPICES

Salt-roasting is an ancient technique that enhances the sweetness and texture of many vegetables, including asparagus, beets, and celeriac (to name only a few). The tart flavor of the yogurt works to highlight the sweetness, but the dish is also excellent with fresh goat cheese or a creamy blue cheese. If you have a nice baking dish such as Portuguese or Scandinavian pottery, use it to bring this to the table for the reveal.

SERVES 4

1 lb (454 g) carrots, trimmed and scrubbed

1 Tbsp (15 mL) minced garlic

1 tsp (5 mL) sesame oil

1 tsp (5 mL) Five-Spice Powder (page 81)

2 egg whites

1 cup (250 mL) salt

1 cup (250 mL) plain yogurt

1 tsp (5 mL) lemon zest

Preheat the oven to 350°F (180°C).

Place the carrots in a saucepan of boiling water and blanch for 3 to 4 minutes. Drain and run under cold water to cool. Rub off the skins with a cloth then dry the carrots with paper towel. Place them in a bowl and season with the garlic, sesame oil, and Five-Spice Powder. Toss well to coat.

In a stand mixer fitted with a whisk attachment, whip the egg whites to stiff peaks. With the machine still running, gradually pour in the salt, whisking to mix. In a casserole dish (13- × 9-inch / 33 × 23 cm), add a layer of salted egg white and spread it evenly across the bottom. Top with the carrots and the remainder of the salt mixture. Spread evenly to coat the carrots.

Place in the oven and bake for 1 hour. Remove from the oven and allow to cool slightly. Crack the salt crust and remove the carrots. In a small bowl, mix the yogurt with the lemon zest until smooth. Plate the carrots and drizzle with the lemon yogurt. Serve immediately.

ROASTED SQUASH WEDGES WITH FIVE-SPICE POWDER

Use a firm-fleshed squash like kabocha, kuri, acorn, or butternut for this. A good tool for cutting a squash is a well-made bread knife. The teeth will bite into the skin and make it less likely to slip. Use a rocking motion to cut down through the squash—and remember, the first cut is always the hardest.

SERVES 4–6

1 medium squash
2 Tbsp (30 mL) olive oil
1 Tbsp (15 mL) Five-Spice Powder
(page 81)
Salt and pepper

Preheat the oven to 350°F (180°C).

Cut the squash in half and remove the seeds and pulp. Remove any woody stem and cut the squash into about eight thick wedges. Transfer to a roasting pan and drizzle with the olive oil and Five-Spice Powder. Season well with salt and pepper.

Place in the oven and roast for 20 to 30 minutes, or until the squash is easily pierced with a fork and the edges are beginning to char. Remove from the oven and allow to cool slightly. Transfer to a serving plate and serve immediately.

ROASTED POTATOES WITH OLIVE OIL AND SPANISH SPICES

These are tapas-worthy potatoes that are crispy on the outside and fluffy on the inside. Russet is the best choice for crispy potatoes, but many other white-, red-, and yellow-skinned potatoes also work well. If the potatoes are smooth-skinned and washed well, you can leave the skins on.

SERVES 4–6

2 lb (900 g) russet potatoes, peeled and washed
3 Tbsp (45 mL) olive oil
1 Tbsp (15 mL) minced fresh sage
1 tsp (5 mL) Spanish Seasoning Powder (page 85)
Salt and pepper

Preheat the oven to 350°F (180°C).

On a cutting board, cut the potatoes into ½-inch (1.25 cm) slices. Place them in a pot of boiling water and bring back to a boil. Turn down the heat to a simmer and cook for 10 minutes, or until the potatoes are just tender. Drain and allow to cool enough to handle.

Transfer the potato slices to a roasting pan and sprinkle them with the oil, sage, spice powder, salt, and pepper. Toss the potatoes to coat and place in the oven. Roast until the potatoes are golden and crispy on the bottom, about 30 minutes. Transfer to a serving bowl and serve warm.

ROASTED NUGGET POTATOES WITH MUSHROOM CURRY POWDER

Use small nugget potatoes for this dish: thin-skinned varieties like purple potatoes, fingerlings, and Warba; yellow varieties like German Butterball and Yukon Gold; or red varieties like All Red or Candy Cane. Young nuggets are often waxy, which results in a creamy texture when they are roasted.

SERVES 4–6

2 lb (900 g) nugget potatoes, washed and drained

2 Tbsp (30 mL) grapeseed oil

1 Tbsp (15 mL) Mushroom Curry Powder (page 82)

Salt and pepper

Preheat the oven to 350°F (180°C).

On a roasting pan, place the potatoes and sprinkle them with the oil, curry powder, salt, and pepper. Toss the potatoes to coat them and place them in the oven. Roast for 15 minutes, then stir the potatoes to redistribute the oil and spices. Continue to cook until the skins are browned and wrinkled, about 15 minutes. The potatoes should feel soft when pressed with your finger or a spoon. Remove from the oven, transfer to a serving bowl, and serve warm.

ROASTED CAULIFLOWER
WITH MISO AND GINGER

You can use slices, florets, or whole cauliflower for this recipe. Bake the dish until the surface is bubbling and slightly charred. This is great as an appetizer with bread or as a side dish with a bigger meal.

SERVES 4–6

1 head cauliflower, trimmed, cored, and cut according to choice
½ cup (125 mL) mayonnaise
2 Tbsp (30 mL) miso paste
2 Tbsp (30 mL) minced pickled ginger
1 Tbsp (15 mL) brown sugar
1 Tbsp (15 mL) light soy sauce
1 Tbsp (15 mL) rice vinegar
4 green onions, trimmed and minced
1 red chili, seeded and minced
Salt and pepper
Micro greens, for garnish

Preheat the oven to 350°F (180°C).

In a large pot filled with boiling water, add the cauliflower and bring the water back to a boil. Turn down the heat and simmer for 4 to 5 minutes, or until the cauliflower is just barely tender. Drain and set aside until needed.

In a small bowl, combine the mayonnaise, miso, ginger, brown sugar, soy sauce, and vinegar with the green onions and chili. Whisk to mix and season with salt and pepper if needed.

Place the cauliflower in an oiled casserole dish (13- × 9-inch/ 33 × 23 cm) and top with the miso mixture. Toss to coat. Place in the oven and bake for 20 minutes, or until the top is golden and beginning to brown. Garnish the top with a few sprigs of micro greens or fresh sprouts. Serve warm.

BAKED PORTOBELLO MUSHROOMS WITH TRUFFLE-CARAMELIZED ONIONS AND GRUYÈRE CHEESE

I have a few uses for Portobello mushrooms, but stuffing and baking seem to be what they are best suited for. Choose mushrooms that are plump and just losing the veil on their underside. Fresh mushrooms should have pink or light chocolate brown gills.

MAKES 6

1 Tbsp (15 mL) butter

2 onions, peeled, trimmed and sliced

Salt and pepper

2 tsp (10 mL) truffle honey (or honey with truffle paste added to taste)

1 cup (250 mL) dry white wine

1 Tbsp (15 mL) minced fresh rosemary

1 Tbsp (15 mL) sherry vinegar

6 large Portobello mushrooms

1 cup (250 mL) grated Gruyère cheese

Preheat the oven to 350°F (180°C).

Place a skillet over medium-high heat and add the butter then the onions. Season with salt and pepper, sauté until the onions just begin to brown, and then add the honey. When the honey melts and begins to caramelize, add the wine and rosemary. Add the sherry vinegar and reduce until all the liquid has evaporated. Remove from the heat and allow to cool.

On a cutting board, snap off the mushroom stems and use a spoon to remove some of the gills. Fill each mushroom with the onion mixture. Top with the cheese and place on a roasting pan. Place in the oven and roast for 20 minutes, or until the mushrooms soften and the cheese bubbles and begins to brown. Remove from the oven and allow to cool slightly. Transfer to a serving plate and serve immediately.

ROASTED FENNEL WITH OLIVES

Fennel has lots of fibre that benefits from a quick blanch in boiling water. Roasting the fennel produces a sweet, caramelized exterior and creamy interior. Use a variety of pitted olives—green, red, and black are all excellent.

SERVES 4–6

3 bulbs fennel, trimmed

1 cup (250 mL) whole pitted olives

4 Tbsp (60 mL) olive oil

1 tsp (5 mL) Spanish Seasoning
    Powder (page 85)

1 tsp (5 mL) hot sauce

Salt and pepper

On a cutting board, trim any dark green tips from the fennel bulbs, leaving only the light green and white parts. Cut each bulb into quarters and shave off a little of the solid core, leaving enough behind to keep the leaves together.

Place the fennel in a pot of boiling water and bring the water back to a boil. Turn down the heat to a simmer and cook for 2 to 3 minutes to partially cook the fennel. Drain and allow to cool enough to handle.

Transfer the fennel to a roasting pan and sprinkle it with the olives, oil, spice powder, and hot sauce. Season with salt and pepper and toss to coat. Place it in the oven and roast until the fennel is crispy and golden on the edges, about 20 minutes. Transfer to a serving bowl and serve warm.

STUFFED PEPPERS WITH CORN, RICE, AND EGG WITH A SOY-GINGER SAUCE

These stuffed peppers are reminiscent of a popular dim sum item that is usually made with shrimp or fish mousse. The egg binds the rice and vegetables and gives a nice texture contrast against the sweet peppers. You can also use the Corn and Black Bean Sauce (page 98) with delicious results. Cook ⅔ cups (160 mL) of rice with 1⅓ cups (310 mL) of water to yield 2 cups (500 mL) of cooked rice. Use any type of rice with this recipe—it's a perfect way to use up leftover rice.

MAKES 6

3 red bell peppers

2 cups (500 mL) cooked rice

1 cup (250 mL) cooked (or frozen) corn kernels

2 eggs, beaten

2 Tbsp (30 mL) minced cilantro

Salt and pepper

2 Tbsp (30 mL) olive oil

1 cup (250 mL) Aromatic Vegetable Stock (page 90) (or water)

2 Tbsp (30 mL) light soy sauce

1 Tbsp (15 mL) minced ginger

1 tsp (5 mL) sesame oil

1 tsp (5 mL) hot sauce

2 green onions, trimmed and minced

1 Tbsp (15 mL) tapioca starch (or cornstarch)

Preheat the oven to 350°F (180°C).

On a cutting board, cut the peppers in half lengthwise and remove the seeds and membrane. Place in a roasting pan and set aside. In a mixing bowl, combine the cooked rice, corn, eggs, and cilantro. Season well with salt and pepper and stir to combine. Fill each of the pepper shells with the rice mixture and drizzle the peppers with olive oil. Place in the oven and bake for 20 minutes, or until the peppers soften and the filling browns on top.

Meanwhile, in a saucepan, combine the stock, soy sauce, ginger, sesame oil, and hot sauce with the green onions. Bring to a boil, turn down the heat to a simmer, and simmer for 2 to 3 minutes. Mix the tapioca starch with enough water to make a thin paste. Add the paste to the boiling sauce and whisk until thickened. Remove the sauce from the heat and keep warm.

Transfer the roasted peppers to a serving platter and pour the sauce overtop. Serve warm.

STUFFED JAPANESE EGGPLANT WITH TOFU AND MISO-GARLIC SAUCE

Japanese eggplant is delicate and sweet, and usually has no hint of the bitterness that comes with other members of the eggplant family. It does tend to collapse when cooked, though, so be careful when plating and serving the final results. Use a long spatula to ease the finished product onto the plate.

SERVES 4–6

3 Japanese eggplants

1 cup (250 mL) soft tofu, diced

2 Tbsp (30 mL) minced garlic, separated

1 Tbsp (15 mL) soy sauce

1 tsp (5 mL) brown sugar

1 cup (250 mL) Aromatic Vegetable Stock (page 90) (or water)

1 medium onion, peeled and chopped

2 Tbsp (30 mL) miso paste

1 tsp (5 mL) sesame oil

1 tsp (5 mL) hot sauce

1 Tbsp (15 mL) tapioca starch (or cornstarch)

1 Tbsp (15 mL) toasted sesame seeds for garnish

Preheat the oven to 350°F (180°C).

On a cutting board, cut each eggplant in half lengthwise. With a small spoon, press down on the centre of the eggplant, creating a groove. Place the eggplant halves on a rimmed baking tray and set aside.

In a small bowl, combine the tofu, 1 tablespoon (15 mL) of the garlic, soy sauce, and brown sugar. Spoon a little tofu mixture onto the centre of each eggplant. Transfer the eggplant to the oven and roast until soft and collapsed, 15 to 20 minutes. Remove from the oven and place the tray on a cooling rack.

Meanwhile, in a saucepan, combine the stock with the onion, miso, the remaining 1 tablespoon (15 mL) garlic, sesame oil, and hot sauce. Bring to a boil, turn down the heat to a simmer, and simmer for 10 minutes. Mix the tapioca starch with enough water to make a thin paste. Add this paste to the boiling sauce and whisk until thickened. Remove the sauce from the heat and keep warm.

Transfer the roasted eggplant to a serving platter and pour the sauce overtop. Sprinkle with toasted sesame seeds and serve warm.

BAKED ACORN SQUASH
WITH PORCINI CUSTARD

Use small squash about the size of a softball. Be careful when halving the squash. I use a sharp bread knife to bite into the skin before pushing down to split the squash open. You can also use this knife to remove a little of the round side of the squash to allow it to sit securely on the baking tray. Make sure not to cut through the flesh to expose the hollow interior.

SERVES 2–4

1 small acorn squash

2 Tbsp (30 mL) olive oil

Salt and pepper

1 cup (250 mL) whipping cream

2 eggs, beaten

1 Tbsp (15 mL) porcini powder

Pinch freshly ground nutmeg

Preheat the oven to 350°F (180°C).

On a cutting board, cut the squash in half, and remove and discard the seeds, pulp, and any woody stem. Place on a rimmed baking tray, drizzle with olive oil, and season with salt and pepper. Place in the oven and roast for 20 minutes, or until the squash is easily pierced with a knife and the edges of the squash are beginning to char. Remove from the oven and allow to cool slightly.

In a bowl, whisk together the cream, eggs, porcini powder, and nutmeg and season well with salt and pepper. Pour the mixture into the squash halves and return to the oven. Bake for about 20 minutes, or until the custard is set around the edges (and jiggling a little in the centre). Allow to cool slightly and serve warm.

GRILLING
AND
SMOKING

CHARRED EGGPLANT WITH OLIVE AND LEMON YOGURT

Eggplant turns into a sensual smooth purée when roasted, and the yogurt helps to balance its richness. This is a great dish to serve with roti, pita, or rustic crusty bread.

SERVES 4

4 medium eggplants

1 cup (250 mL) Greek-style yogurt

1 lemon, juice and zest

1 Tbsp (15 mL) honey

1 Tbsp (15 mL) chopped fresh
    flat-leaf parsley (or cilantro)

1 tsp (5 mL) minced garlic

Salt and pepper

¼ cup (65 mL) minced, pitted olives

Olive oil, for drizzling

Preheat the grill to 400°F (200°C).

Place the whole eggplants on the hot grill and char on all sides. The eggplants will collapse slightly when cooked and the skin will be blistered and charred. Carefully remove to a platter. Hold one eggplant by the stem and scrape off the charred skin with a knife. Place in a bowl, repeat with the remaining eggplants, cover with plastic wrap, and keep warm.

In a small bowl, combine the yogurt, lemon juice and zest, honey, parsley, and garlic. Season with salt and pepper and set aside.

To serve, gently place one whole eggplant on a plate and top with a large dollop of the yogurt. Sprinkle with the minced olives, drizzle with olive oil, and serve warm or at room temperature.

CHARRED LEEKS WITH GARLIC-HERB BUTTER

Leeks are transformed on the grill into something magical with a bit of char and a rich coating of butter and garlic. Feel free to vary the herbs and cheese to suit your taste. These are also great with a soft ripened cheese like Brie or Camembert.

SERVES 4

4 large leeks, trimmed, split lengthwise, and washed
1 Tbsp (15 mL) olive oil
1 tsp (5 mL) Spanish Seasoning Powder (page 85)
Salt and pepper
4 slices rustic bread
¼ cup (65 mL) butter
2 Tbsp (30 mL) chopped garlic
1 Tbsp (15 mL) minced fresh sage
1 Tbsp (15 mL) minced fresh thyme
1 Tbsp (15 mL) chopped fresh flat-leaf parsley
½ lemon, juice and zest
Aged sheep cheese (or Parmesan), for garnish

Preheat the grill to 400°F (200°C).

On a plate or tray, place the leeks and drizzle them with the olive oil. Sprinkle with the spice powder and season with salt and pepper. Place them on the hot grill and cook until charred and beginning to soften. Place the bread on the grill and toast on both sides. Place the leeks and toasted bread on a platter and keep warm while you make the sauce.

In a sauté pan over medium heat, place the butter then the garlic, sage, thyme, and parsley. Stir to melt and cook until the butter sizzles and the garlic just begins to brown. Add the lemon juice and zest and swirl to mix. Remove from the heat and keep warm.

To serve, place a toasted bread slice on a plate, top with charred leek and drizzle with a little garlic butter. Grate a little sheep cheese on top and around the plate and grind a little freshly ground black pepper on top. Serve immediately.

GRILLED CAULIFLOWER WITH SPICED RAISIN SAUCE

The cauliflower is a beautiful plant. Cutting the vegetable in slices gives a cross-section of the head and creates lots of surface area to char and develop flavors. You can use a wide variety of cauliflower types like white, orange, green, or Romanesco.

SERVES 4

1 head cauliflower, trimmed

1 Tbsp (15 mL) olive oil

1 Tbsp (15 mL) minced garlic

Salt and pepper

1 cup (250 mL) Aromatic Vegetable
  Stock (page 90) (or water)

¼ cup (65 mL) golden raisins, soaked
  in 1 cup (250 mL) boiling water

1 stalk celery, trimmed and
  finely diced

2 Tbsp (30 mL) red wine vinegar

1 Tbsp (15 mL) Mushroom Curry
  Powder (page 82)

1 Tbsp (15 mL) orange marmalade

1 tsp (5 mL) minced ginger

1 Tbsp (15 mL) minced cilantro

2 tsp (10 mL) tapioca starch
  (or cornstarch)

Preheat the grill to 400°F (200°C).

On a cutting board, remove the stem of the cauliflower to allow the head to sit flat on the surface. Cut the cauliflower into ½-inch (1.25 cm) slices. Place them on a tray and drizzle with the olive oil (to lightly coat), garlic, salt, and pepper. Toss gently to coat.

Place the cauliflower on the hot grill and char on both sides, 5 to 7 minutes per side. Carefully place the pieces on a platter, using tongs or a spatula. Keep warm until needed.

In a saucepan over medium heat, bring the stock to a boil. Drain the raisins and add them to the pot along with the celery, vinegar, curry powder, marmalade, and ginger. Turn down the heat to a simmer and cook for 5 minutes. Add the cilantro. In a small bowl, mix the tapioca starch with enough cold water to make a thin paste. Add this to the boiling sauce and whisk to mix and thicken.

To serve, place the cauliflower on a serving platter and top with the raisin sauce. Serve immediately.

GRILLED PUMPKIN WITH SWEET AND SOUR SAUCE

Pumpkin is used in savory applications all over the planet. Grilling helps to concentrate the flavor and removes some of the moisture from the flesh. This helps to accentuate both the sweetness and the luxurious texture.

SERVES 4

1 small winter pumpkin

1 Tbsp (15 mL) olive oil

1 Tbsp (15 mL) minced garlic

1 tsp (5 mL) Five-Spice Powder
(page 81)

Salt and pepper

1 cup (250 mL) Aromatic Vegetable
Stock (page 90) (or water)

1 cup (250 mL) tomato juice

2 Tbsp (30 mL) cider vinegar

1 Tbsp (15 mL) maple syrup

1 Tbsp (15 mL) minced ginger

1 Tbsp (15 mL) minced basil leaves

2 tsp (10 mL) tapioca starch
(or cornstarch)

Preheat the grill to 400°F (200°C).

Cut the pumpkin in half and remove the seeds and membrane. Cut into wedges (1 inch / 2.5 cm thick) and place on a rimmed baking tray. Drizzle with the olive oil and season with the garlic, spice powder, salt, and pepper. Place the pumpkin pieces on the hot grill and char on both sides, 8 to 10 minutes per side. Finish by placing the pumpkin skin-side down on the grill for 3 to 4 minutes. Carefully place the pumpkin pieces on a platter, using tongs or a spatula. Keep warm until needed.

In a saucepan over medium heat, add the stock, tomato juice, vinegar, maple syrup, and ginger. Bring to a boil, turn down the heat to a simmer, and cook for 5 minutes. Add the basil and stir to mix.

In a small bowl, mix the tapioca starch with enough cold water to make a thin paste. Add to the boiling sauce and whisk to mix and thicken.

To serve, place the pumpkin on a serving platter and top with the sweet and sour sauce. Serve immediately.

GRILLED ASPARAGUS WITH STINGING NETTLE AND HAZELNUT PESTO

Springtime is the only time for asparagus. Stinging nettles are poking up at the same time, so they are a natural pairing. When collecting nettles, use gloves to avoid being stung. At home, wash the nettles with cold water and drain. Blanching the nettles first will remove the sting from the leaves. Both the asparagus and nettles offer a lot of intense flavor and the notes of lemon and hazelnut help to add complexity and balance. If you don't want to use nuts, you can use pumpkin seeds or sunflower seeds.

SERVES 4

2 cups (500 mL) stinging nettles
   (or kale or spinach)
½ cup (125 mL) toasted hazelnuts
1 lemon, juice and zest
3 Tbsp (45 mL) olive oil
1 tsp (5 mL) sesame oil
1 tsp (5 mL) minced garlic
1 lb (454 g) asparagus
1 Tbsp (15 mL) melted butter
Salt and pepper
Olive oil, for garnish

Preheat the grill to 400°F (200°C).

Bring a pot of water to boil over high heat. Add the stinging nettles and cook for 2 to 3 minutes. Remove them from the hot water and plunge into a bowl of cold water. Strain and squeeze the nettles with your hands to remove as much moisture as possible. Coarsely chop the nettles and place in the bowl of a food processor. Add the hazelnuts and pulse to form a coarse paste. Add the lemon juice and zest, olive oil, sesame oil, and garlic. Process until a chunky purée is reached. Season with salt and pepper and set aside until needed.

On a plate, combine the asparagus and melted butter (or olive oil). Season with salt and pepper. Place the asparagus on the hot grill and char for about 5 minutes per side. Remove to a bowl and keep warm. Add a couple of spoonfuls of the pesto to the bowl and stir to coat. Transfer to a serving plate and drizzle a little pesto around the plate. Finish with a drizzle of olive oil.

GRILLED BOK CHOY WITH MUSHROOM AND BLACK BEAN VINAIGRETTE

Grilling Asian vegetables like bok choy, gai lan, and gai choy adds a charred bitterness that works to highlight the sweetness of the vegetable. Use your favorite mushrooms and sauté them quickly in a little grapeseed oil before cooling and mincing. Black beans are salted. To remove excess salt, place the beans in warm water for 2 to 3 minutes then drain before continuing with the recipe.

SERVES 4

6 baby bok choy, rinsed

1 Tbsp (15 mL) olive oil

Salt and pepper

2 green onions, trimmed and minced

1 cup (250 mL) minced cooked
    mushrooms (button, shiitake,
    shimeji, etc.)

1 Tbsp (15 mL) salted, fermented
    black beans, minced

1 Tbsp (15 mL) minced ginger

1 Tbsp (15 mL) soy sauce

1 Tbsp (15 mL) rice vinegar

1 tsp (5 mL) sesame oil

2 Tbsp (30 mL) grapeseed oil

2 Tbsp (30 mL) chopped cilantro,
    for garnish

Toasted sesame seeds, for garnish

Preheat the grill to 400°F (200°C).

Place the bok choy on a cutting board and trim the ends (but leave most of the stem to keep the leaves together). Discard any leaves that are discolored or damaged. Cut each in half and transfer the bok choy to a plate, drizzle with olive oil, and season with salt and pepper. Place the bok choy on the hot grill and char on all sides. It will cook very quickly, 1 to 2 minutes per side. Slightly char the leaves and cook until the base is just warmed through.

In a small mixing bowl, combine the green onions, mushrooms, black beans, ginger, soy sauce, vinegar, and sesame oil. Whisk to mix well and then add the grapeseed oil in a slow stream, whisking until incorporated and smooth.

To serve, place the bok choy on a serving platter and drizzle with the vinaigrette. Garnish with a sprinkling of cilantro and sesame seeds and serve hot.

GRILLED PORTOBELLO MUSHROOMS STUFFED WITH AVOCADO, GOAT CHEESE, AND TOMATO

Use a ripe avocado for this dish. Portobellos are at their prime when smooth and plump. The gills should be chocolate brown on the fresh specimens. As the mushroom ages, the gills darken to black and the edges split.

SERVES 4

4 large Portobello mushrooms

1 Tbsp (15 mL) minced garlic

1 Tbsp (15 mL) olive oil

Salt and pepper

1 ripe avocado

2 ripe tomatoes

1 Tbsp (15 mL) balsamic vinegar

¼ cup (65 mL) crumbled fresh
    goat cheese

1 Tbsp (15 mL) chopped fresh basil,
    mint, or cilantro

Extra olive oil, for finishing

Preheat the grill to 400°F (200°C).

On a cutting board, snap off the stem of the mushrooms (they should snap off easily). If the gills are very dark, remove as much as possible with a spoon. Sprinkle the inside of the mushrooms with the garlic and olive oil. Season well with salt and pepper and place on the hot grill. Cook until the mushrooms wilt slightly and the bases are browned and just beginning to char, about 5 minutes. Transfer to a plate and keep warm.

On a cutting board, slice the avocado lengthwise and split it in half to reveal the pit. Remove the pit and skin and cut out any discolored sections. Chop the avocado into chunks and place them in a small bowl. Core the tomatoes, cut them in half, and then dice. Add the tomato dice to the avocado, drizzle with balsamic vinegar, and season with salt and pepper.

Mound the avocado mixture into the mushrooms and top with the crumbled goat cheese. Garnish with chopped herbs and a drizzle of good olive oil. Serve warm or at room temperature.

SMOKED SHIITAKE MUSHROOMS WITH LEEKS, PEPPERS, AND KOREAN FLAVORS

This dish works with many types of wild and cultivated mushrooms. You can also use a mix of mushrooms for a nice effect. Gochujang is a spicy Korean paste made from fermented soy, rice, and chilies (and sometimes other ingredients like barley, pumpkin, and sweet potato). You can substitute miso for gochujang with good results. I use a wire cooling rack for convenience when smoking (the produce is evenly supported and does not fall through the gaps), but you can also use the wider racks that come with most home smokers.

SERVES 4

1 Tbsp (15 mL) soy sauce

1 tsp (5 mL) hot sauce

1 tsp (5 mL) honey

1 lb (454 g) shiitake mushrooms

2 Tbsp (30 mL) grapeseed oil

1 Tbsp (15 mL) minced ginger

4 green onions, trimmed
   and chopped

1 leek, trimmed, split lengthwise,
   and washed

1 red bell pepper, cored and cubed

1 red chili, seeded and minced

2 Tbsp (30 mL) gochujang or
   miso paste

1 Tbsp (15 mL) minced garlic

Toasted sesame seeds, for garnish

Preheat the smoker to 150°F (65°C).

In a bowl, combine the soy sauce, hot sauce, and honey. Stir to mix and dissolve the honey. Add the mushrooms and toss to coat. Allow to sit for 15 minutes, turning occasionally. Drain the mushrooms and place them on a wire rack, and put them in the smoker for about 1 hour. Remove and keep warm until needed.

In a sauté pan, place the oil and then the ginger and stir until fragrant. Add the green onions, leek, bell pepper, chili, gochujang, and garlic. Sauté to warm through and to slightly char the vegetables. Add the mushrooms and toss to coat. Transfer to a serving plate and garnish with toasted sesame seeds. Serve warm or at room temperature.

SMOKED BEETS WITH LIME, OLIVES, FETA, AND JALAPEÑO

Beets take on a subtle, and dare I say meaty, flavor when introduced to smoke. Cut smaller beets into wedges. Large beets can be smoked whole and cut into thin slices. Use your favorite olives (or a mix) for this dish.

SERVES 4–6

2 lb (about 900 g) small beets

1 Tbsp (15 mL) olive oil

Salt and pepper

½ cup (125 mL) crumbled feta cheese, rinsed

¼ cup (65 mL) chopped, pitted olives

1 jalapeño pepper, seeded and minced

2 Tbsp (30 mL) minced shallots

1 lime, juice and zest

1 Tbsp (15 mL) chopped cilantro (or fresh dill)

Olive oil, to garnish

Preheat the smoker to 150°F (65°C).

In a large pot, cover the beets with cold water. Bring to a boil over high heat, then turn down the heat and simmer for 20 to 30 minutes, or until the beets are easily pierced by a small knife. Drain and allow to cool just enough to handle. They should still be warm.

Peel the warm beets, cut in quarters, and place in a bowl. Drizzle with olive oil and season with salt and pepper. Transfer the beets to a wire rack, cut side down, and place the rack in the smoker. Smoke for 1 hour then remove, place in a mixing bowl, and keep warm until needed.

To serve, add the feta, olives, jalapeño, shallots, and lime juice and zest to the bowl and toss to mix. Taste and then season with salt and pepper if necessary. Transfer to a serving plate and top with the chopped cilantro and a drizzle of olive oil. Serve warm or at room temperature.

SMOKED MIXED ONION GRATIN WITH AGED SHEEP MILK

This gratin works with a wide variety of bulb onions: red, sweet, cipollini, and pearl are all excellent. A nice mix of sizes and colors makes a wonderful presentation. Use an aged sheep milk cheese like Manchego, or seek out some of the local artisan cheeses now being made across North America. Roughly 1.5 cups (375 mL) of rice cooked with 3 cups (750 mL) of water will yield about 4 cups (1 L) of cooked rice.

SERVES 4

2 lb (about 1 kg) mixed onions

2 Tbsp (30 mL) butter

2 Tbsp (30 mL) all-purpose flour

2 cups (500 mL) milk

1 Tbsp (15 mL) Spanish Seasoning Powder (page 85)

2 cups (500 mL) shredded sheep milk cheese, divided

4 cups (1 L) cooked rice (short-grain white or brown)

Preheat the smoker to 150°F (65°C).

In a large pot of salted boiling water, cook the onions for 4 to 5 minutes. Remove them with a slotted spoon and place them in a bowl of cold water. Peel off the outer layer of skin and trim off any root visible. Cut them in half (or quarters if they're large) and place them on a wire rack. Place the rack in the smoker and leave for 1 hour. Remove from the smoker and reserve until needed.

Preheat the oven to 350°F (180°C).

In a saucepan over medium heat, melt the butter. Toss in the flour and whisk to incorporate. Add ½ cup (125 mL) of the milk and quickly mix to dissolve lumps and leave a smooth paste. The paste will thicken as it cooks. Add another ¾ cup (180 mL) of milk and whisk until smooth. Add the remaining milk and whisk to blend. Turn down the heat and simmer, stirring occasionally, until the mixture thickens, about 5 minutes. Add the spice powder and 1 cup (250 mL) of the cheese. Stir to melt the cheese. Remove from the heat and set aside until needed.

In an oiled casserole dish (13- × 9-inch / 33 × 23 cm), place the onions and cover them with the cheese sauce. Top with the remaining cheese and place in the oven for 30 minutes, or until the top is bubbling and browned. Remove from the oven and allow to cool slightly. Serve warm with plenty of rustic bread or as a topping for rice or potatoes.

SMOKED CARROTS WITH SESAME AND PLUM

This may seem like a bit of a project, but smoke adds something wonderful to the humble carrot by bringing out its sweetness. It also works well with the nuttiness of the sesame seeds.

SERVES 4

2 lb (about 1 kg) carrots,
    peeled and trimmed
1 Tbsp (15 mL) olive oil
1 Tbsp (15 mL) honey
1 Tbsp (15 mL) Five-Spice Powder
    (page 81)
1 tsp (5 mL) salt
1 cup (250 mL) chopped, pitted
    plums (prune or red plum)
1 Tbsp (15 mL) minced
    pickled ginger
1 Tbsp (15 mL) mirin
1 tsp (5 mL) sesame oil
¼ cup (65 mL) raw sesame seeds

Preheat the smoker to 150°F (65°C).

Place the carrots on a rimmed baking tray and drizzle them with the olive oil, honey, Five-Spice Powder, and salt. Toss well to coat and allow to sit for 15 minutes, turning occasionally. Transfer the carrots to a cooling rack and allow to dry slightly then place the rack in the smoker for about 2 hours. Remove from the heat and allow to cool.

In a small pot, combine the chopped plums, ginger, mirin, and sesame oil. Bring to a boil, turn down the heat, and simmer until the mixture softens. Purée with an immersion blender and simmer until the mixture reduces to a paste, 15 to 20 minutes. Strain into a small bowl, pressing down with the back of a ladle or spoon to extract all the juice.

In a dry sauté pan over medium-high heat, add the sesame seeds and toast them until golden brown. Transfer them to a plate, let cool, and then grind them coarsely in a coffee or spice grinder. Return them to the plate.

Place the carrots on a separate plate and drizzle with enough plum purée to cover them. Take one carrot and roll it in the ground sesame seeds. Transfer to a serving plate and repeat with the remaining carrots. Drizzle a little plum sauce around the plate and serve at room temperature.

SIDES
AND
STIR-FRIES

SOUS VIDE POACHED CARROTS WITH SPANISH SEASONING POWDER AND OLIVE OIL

Sous vide is a technique that literally means "under vacuum." It usually refers to a technique where food is placed in a bag, seasoned, and sealed by a vacuum sealer. Modern commercial kitchens also use a device called a thermal immersion circulator to create a consistent heat to break down fibres, make the food tender, and preserve nutrients and vitamins.

SERVES 4

1 lb (454 g) baby carrots, washed and scrubbed

1 Tbsp (15 mL) olive oil

1 shallot, peeled, trimmed, and minced

1 Tbsp (15 mL) minced garlic

1 tsp (5 mL) Spanish Seasoning Powder (page 85)

Salt and pepper

Place the cleaned carrots in a vacuum bag. Season with the olive oil, shallot, garlic, spice powder, salt, and pepper.

Place the bag in a vacuum machine (follow the machine directions) and allow the machine to extract air and heat-seal the bag. Alternatively, you can place the contents in a resealable plastic bag and use a straw to extract most of the air before quickly sealing it.

Place the bag in a pot of hot water held at 194°F (90°C) using an immersion circulator. Cook for 20 to 25 minutes, or until the carrots yield to light pressure when squeezed. Remove the bag from the water bath and allow to cool slightly. Cut open the bag and pour the contents onto a serving plate. Alternatively, you can place the bag in barely simmering water (about 200°F/95°C) for 18 to 20 minutes. Remove from the heat and allow to cool slightly before opening.

MASHED POTATOES WITH VARIATIONS

Use baking or russet potatoes for the lightest and fluffiest mashed potatoes. Use a potato ricer (a potato press) or a food mill to squeeze the potato into a paste. Using a mixer overworks the potato and gummy starches will develop. Lightly working the potato will give you an incredibly silky mash.

SERVES 4

2 lb (about 1 kg) russet potatoes, scrubbed

1 tsp (5 mL) salt

¼ cup (65 mL) whipping cream (or milk), warmed

4 Tbsp (60 mL) butter

Salt and pepper

Rinse the potatoes and place them in a large saucepan of lightly salted cold water. Bring to a boil, turn down the heat to medium, and cook for 20 minutes, or until all the potatoes are easily pierced with a fork.

Drain the potatoes and let cool enough to handle and peel them. While they're still warm, mash them with a ricer, food mill, or masher. Return them to the saucepan and add the cream and butter. Stir well to mix until smooth and creamy. Season well with salt and pepper.

These can be made in advance and kept warm until needed (cover and hold for up to 1 hour in a warm oven). If the potato firms up, thin it with a little warm cream or milk until a soft mash is obtained. Serve warm.

VARIATIONS (ADD TO THE FINISHED MASH):

- Roasted garlic: add 2 Tbsp (30 mL) minced
- Truffle paste: add 1 tsp (5 mL)
- Cheese (blue, goat, cheddar, Parmesan, etc): add ¼ cup (65 mL) crumbled or grated
- Horseradish: add 1 Tbsp (15 mL) fresh grated
- Miso: add 1 Tbsp (15 mL)
- Sour cream: add ¼ cup (65 mL)
- Pesto (basil, spinach, stinging nettle, etc.): add 2 Tbsp (30 mL)
- Smoked mushroom: add ½ cup (125 mL) minced
- Onion (green, caramelized, smoked, etc.): add ½ cup (125 mL) chopped
- Spice powder (Five-Spice Powder, Mushroom Curry Powder, Spanish Seasoning Powder [pages 81–85]): add 1 tsp (5 mL) or to taste

BRAISED POTATO WITH KALE AND MUSHROOM CURRY POWDER

This is a fairly classic preparation, elevated by the Mushroom Curry Powder. You could also try adding morels or other mushrooms to the mix. Kale is an excellent choice, but you could also use spinach, pea tips, mustard greens, or green cabbage.

SERVES 4

2 lb (about 1 kg) russet potatoes, peeled

2 cups (500 mL) Aromatic Vegetable Stock (page 90) (or water)

1 Tbsp (15 mL) Mushroom Curry Powder (page 82)

1 Tbsp (15 mL) minced ginger

1 Tbsp (15 mL) minced garlic

4 cups (1 L) shredded kale leaves (stems removed)

1 cup (250 mL) Greek-style yogurt (or coconut milk)

Salt and pepper

Preheat the oven to 350°F (180°C).

Cut the potatoes into ½-inch (1.25 cm) dice. Place them in a casserole dish (13- × 9-inch / 33 × 23 cm) and cover with the stock. Add the curry powder, ginger, and garlic. Place in the oven and braise for 30 minutes, or until the potato is just tender. Add the kale leaves and stir to mix. Return to the oven and bake for another 10 minutes, stirring occasionally.

Add the yogurt and stir it into the vegetables. Return the potatoes to the oven to warm through, about 5 minutes. Taste, and season with salt and pepper if necessary. Serve warm.

SQUASH GNOCCHI WITH ROASTED TOMATOES, GARLIC, OLIVE OIL, AND HERBS

Butternut and banana squash are mild and sweet varieties that work well as gnocchi. Roast the squash and the tomato mixture at the same time. Use a meaty tomato like Roma or Bull's Heart. Remove the skin from the squash before dicing.

SERVES 4–6

1 lb (454 g) russet potatoes, scrubbed

2 cups (500 mL) cherry tomatoes

¼ cup (65 mL) olive oil

2 Tbsp (30 mL) minced fresh sage

2 Tbsp (30 mL) shredded fresh basil

1 Tbsp (15 mL) minced garlic

1 tsp (5 mL) hot sauce

Salt and pepper

4 cups (1 L) cubed squash

2 Tbsp (30 mL) olive oil

1½ cups (375 mL) all-purpose flour

1 egg, beaten

1 tsp (5 mL) salt

2 Tbsp (30 mL) grapeseed
   (or olive) oil

¼ cup (65 mL) grated
   Parmesan cheese

Cook the potatoes in a large pot of boiling water until soft, 30 to 40 minutes. A knife should easily pierce the flesh. Drain and allow to cool slightly.

Meanwhile, on a rimmed baking tray, combine the tomatoes, ¼ cup (65 mL) olive oil, sage, basil, garlic, and hot sauce. Season well with salt and pepper and place in the oven. Bake until the tomatoes burst, the skin lightly chars, and the garlic is tender, about 30 minutes.

On a separate rimmed baking tray, spread out the squash cubes and drizzle them with the 2 Tbsp (30 mL) olive oil. Season with salt and pepper and place in the oven with the tomatoes for 20 minutes, or until soft and just starting to brown.

Transfer the tomato mix to a saucepan, scraping the tray clean with a spatula. Set aside until needed.

While the potatoes are still warm, peel and cube them and pass them and the roasted squash cubes through a vegetable mill (or potato ricer) onto a clean, floured work surface. Sprinkle the 1½ cups (375 mL) flour over the riced potato and squash. Make a well in the centre, add the egg and 1 tsp (5 mL) salt, and stir them into the vegetable mixture. Bring the dough together, kneading gently until a ball is formed. Let sit for 10 minutes.

Preheat the oven to 350°F (180°C).

Roll a baseball-sized ball of dough into a 1-inch (2.5 cm) thick log and cut the log into square pieces. With floured hands, roll each piece into a ball and flatten slightly with a fork. Cook the gnocchi in batches in a large pot of boiling water. As the dough cooks it will begin to float. Cook for 1 minute more and then transfer to a bowl of cold water. Repeat with the remaining dough. Once the gnocchi has cooled, drain it and panfry in a little oil or butter until just browned, about 10 minutes. To serve, reheat the sauce, place the gnocchi in a pasta bowl, and top with sauce and a sprinkle of Parmesan.

RED LENTIL DAL WITH CARAMELIZED ENDIVE, CARROT, AND TOMATO

Red lentils break down into a pleasant mix of earthy and rich flavors that marries well with spices and vegetables. Making your own spice mix pays huge dividends in this recipe. Thick-fleshed tomatoes like Roma or beefsteak work well in this recipe. Dal is traditionally served over brown rice or eaten with a flatbread like naan or pita.

SERVES 4

4 Belgian endives, washed

2 tomatoes, cored and diced

1 carrot, peeled, trimmed, and diced

1 red chili, seeded and minced

1 Tbsp (15 mL) grapeseed oil

Salt and pepper

1 cup (250 mL) red lentils, washed

2 cups (500 mL) Aromatic Vegetable Stock (page 90) (or water)

1 Tbsp (15 mL) minced ginger

1 Tbsp (15 mL) minced garlic

1 Tbsp (15 mL) Mushroom Curry Powder (page 82)

3 Tbsp (45 mL) chopped cilantro

Preheat the oven to 350°F (180°C).

Trim the stem end from the endives, and cut the endives in half lengthwise and then in strips. Dice the strips. Place the endive dice on a rimmed baking tray and add the tomatoes, carrot, and chili. Drizzle with the oil and season well with salt and pepper. Toss to coat and place in the oven. Roast until browned on the cut edge, about 20 minutes.

In a saucepan over medium heat, combine the lentils with the stock, ginger, garlic, and curry powder. Bring to a boil then turn down the heat to a simmer. Using a rubber spatula, scrape the contents of the baking tray into the pot. Simmer until the lentils have softened and are starting to break down and thicken the sauce. It should take on the consistency of a thick porridge. Add more stock or water if the mixture becomes too thick. Stir in the cilantro then taste and season with salt and pepper, if necessary. Serve warm.

CREAMED KALE WITH CHICKPEAS, COCONUT MILK, AND LIME

The kale can be blanched ahead of time, squeezed free of all moisture, and stored in a container with a tight-fitting lid until you need it. If you like spicy food, feel free to add a fresh chili or a dose of hot sauce to the dish.

SERVES 4

1 Tbsp (15 mL) grapeseed
   (or coconut) oil

1 onion, peeled, trimmed, and diced

1 Tbsp (15 mL) minced garlic

1 Tbsp (15 mL) Mushroom Curry
   Powder (page 82)

1 cup (250 mL) coconut milk

1 lime, juice and zest

Salt and pepper

1 lb (454 g) kale, washed and
   stems removed

1 cup (250 mL) cooked (or canned)
   chickpeas

2 Tbsp (30 mL) toasted pine nuts

In a large sauté pan over medium heat, heat the oil then sauté the onion until it begins to brown. Add the garlic and curry powder and stir to mix. When the mixture just begins to stick to the bottom of the pan, add the coconut milk and lime juice and zest. Taste, and season with salt and pepper if necessary.

Roll the kale into a log and cut it into thin shreds. Add the kale and chickpeas to the coconut sauce and stir to mix. Cook until the kale softens and becomes tender, about 5 minutes. Transfer to a platter or bowl, garnish with pine nuts, and serve hot.

STEAMED FENNEL WITH GOAT CHEESE SAUCE

When fennel is steamed, fibres break down and the vegetable becomes very creamy. Try to balance a little texture with this quality by removing the fennel from the steamer when it is just barely tender.

SERVES 4

3 bulbs fennel, trimmed

1 Tbsp (15 mL) butter

2 shallots, peeled and trimmed

1 Tbsp (15 mL) minced garlic

1 cup (250 mL) dry white wine

1 cup (250 mL) whipping cream

2 Tbsp (30 mL) minced thyme leaves

¼ cup (65 mL) fresh goat cheese

Salt and pepper

2 Tbsp (30 mL) chopped fresh
    flat-leaf parsley

Trim any dark green tips from the fennel bulbs, leaving only the light green and white parts. Cut each bulb into quarters and shave off a little of the solid core, leaving enough behind to keep the leaves together.

In a saucepan, place the butter and shallots. Heat over medium-high heat until fragrant, add the garlic, and warm through (about 1 minute). Add the white wine and reduce to one-quarter of the original volume. Add the cream and thyme and reduce until the cream thickens slightly, 2 to 3 minutes. Add the goat cheese, remove from the heat, and whisk until smooth. Season with salt and pepper and stir to mix. Set aside until needed.

Place a steamer tray over a pot containing 2 inches (5 cm) of water. Bring the water to a boil, place the fennel in the steamer tray, cover with a lid, and steam until the fennel is tender, 8 to 10 minutes. Be careful not to overcook the fennel.

Reheat the sauce until just warm. Place the fennel on a serving plate and spoon the sauce overtop. Sprinkle with the parsley and serve warm.

STEAMED BRUSSELS SPROUTS WITH BLACK BEAN SAUCE

Choose nice large Brussels sprouts for this dish. There are now purple and varie-gated red varieties available in the market. If the sprouts are large, you can cut an x in the bottom to help ensure even cooking. Be careful not to overcook the sprouts. A knife will slip in easily when they are cooked and the sprouts will still be bright green. Overcooked sprouts will slowly turn olive green and mushy as they continue to cook. The black beans are salted. If you want to remove some salt, rinse the beans quickly under hot running water and strain before adding to the recipe.

SERVES 4

1 Tbsp (15 mL) grapeseed oil

1 onion, peeled, trimmed, and finely diced

1 red bell pepper, seeded and diced

2 Tbsp (30 mL) salted, fermented black beans, minced

1 Tbsp (15 mL) minced ginger

1 Tbsp (15 mL) minced garlic

2 cups (500 mL) Aromatic Vegetable Stock (page 90) (or water)

1 Tbsp (15 mL) soy sauce

1 tsp (5 mL) hot sauce

1 tsp (5 mL) sesame oil

1 Tbsp (15 mL) tapioca starch (or cornstarch)

Salt and pepper

2 lb (900 g) Brussels sprouts, trimmed

2 Tbsp (30 mL) chopped cilantro leaves

Place the oil in a saucepan over medium-high heat and add the onion, red pepper, black beans, ginger, and garlic. Sauté until the onion starts to soften and brown. Add the stock, soy sauce, hot sauce, and sesame oil. Bring to a boil, turn down the heat to a simmer, and cook for 10 minutes, or until all the vegetables are soft. Mix the tapioca starch in a small bowl with enough water to make a thin paste. Stir this into the sauce until it thickens. Taste, and season with salt and pepper if necessary.

Place a steamer pot containing 2 inches (5 cm) of water on the stove. Place the Brussels sprouts in the steamer and cover with a lid. Bring the water to a boil and steam until the sprouts are tender, 7 to 8 minutes.

Transfer to a serving bowl. Top with the black bean sauce, toss to coat, and garnish with the cilantro leaves.

THAI-STYLE STIR-FRIED EGGPLANT WITH HONEY AND GARLIC

Japanese eggplants are very tender, and are creamy and delicious when cooked through. Be careful not to scorch the eggplants as you sauté them. They generally tend to absorb oil like a sponge early in the cooking process and will release some oil as they continue to cook. Don't be tempted to add more oil to the pan.

SERVES 4

2 Tbsp (30 mL) grapeseed oil

2 slices ginger

2 Tbsp (30 mL) minced garlic

1 red chili, seeded and minced

4 Japanese eggplants,
    trimmed and sliced

1 Tbsp (15 mL) honey

1 cup (250 mL) Aromatic Vegetable
    Stock (page 90) or water

2 Tbsp (30 mL) light soy sauce

1 Tbsp (15 mL) shredded fresh Thai
    (or regular) basil

1 Tbsp (15 mL) shredded mint leaves

1 Tbsp (15 mL) tapioca starch
    (or cornstarch)

1 cup (250 mL) mung bean sprouts

¼ cup (65 mL) dry-roasted peanuts,
    for garnish

Basil and mint sprigs, for garnish

In a large sauté pan over high heat, place the grapeseed oil then the ginger, garlic, and chili. Add the eggplant slices and quickly sauté while stirring constantly. (Sauté them in two batches if you have a small sauté pan. Add all the cooked eggplant to the pan and continue with the recipe as if you had cooked it all in one batch.)

When the eggplant just begins to brown, add the honey and toss the pan to melt it. Immediately add the stock and soy sauce. Bring to a boil, turn down the heat to a simmer, and add the basil and mint.

In a small bowl, mix the tapioca starch with enough water to make a thin paste. Add this to the sauce and stir to thicken. When the sauce is thick, add the sprouts and toss to warm through. Immediately transfer the eggplant and sauce to a serving platter and garnish with roasted peanuts and fresh basil and mint sprigs.

SAUTÉED GREEN BEANS WITH SHALLOTS, GARLIC, AND CHILIES

Chinese restaurants make a version of this dish with heaps of dried chili flakes and garlic. You can use many types of chilies—jalapeño for a tangy bite, serrano chilies for more heat, or Thai red chilies for a potent burst of heat. Use your taste buds as your guide and add a little at a time until you have the right heat level. Most of the heat is in the seeds and surrounding membrane of the chili. Adding these will produce the highest levels of heat. The combination of green beans and chilies is truly a magical one. This dish is also excellent with asparagus, gai lan, bok choy, and the Chinese long bean (snake bean or dau gok).

SERVES 4

1 lb (454 g) green beans, trimmed into 4-inch (10 cm) chunks
1 Tbsp (15 mL) grapeseed oil
2 shallots, peeled, trimmed, and diced
1 Tbsp (15 mL) minced garlic
1–2 whole fresh chilies, minced
2 Tbsp (30 mL) chopped cilantro
Salt and pepper

In a large pot of salted, boiling water, cook the beans until bright green and just tender, about 5 minutes. Drain and immediately cool in cold water.

In a sauté pan over high heat, place the grapeseed oil then the shallots, garlic, and chili. When fragrant, add the beans and sauté to cook the beans and slightly blister the skin. Add the cilantro and season very well with salt and pepper. Transfer to a platter and serve immediately.

DESSERTS

BLUEBERRY AND FENNEL COBBLER

Fennel is an interesting vegetable ingredient for desserts. Here it is cooked in a syrup that sweetens and tenderizes the bulb. You can use blueberries, blackberries, raspberries, and even plums, apples, and pears in this interesting dessert.

SERVES 8–10

2 bulbs fennel

1 cup (250 mL) granulated sugar

2 cups (500 mL) blueberries
    (fresh or frozen)

1 Tbsp (15 mL) tapioca starch
    (or cornstarch)

1½ cups (375 mL) all-purpose flour

½ cup (125 mL) brown sugar

1 tsp (5 mL) baking powder

½ cup (125 mL) sour cream

¼ cup (65 mL) melted butter

1 lemon, juice and zest

Trim any dark green tips from the fennel bulbs, leaving only the light green and white parts. Cut each bulb into quarters and shave off a little of the solid core. Dice the fennel and set it aside.

Heat a saucepan over medium heat and add 1 cup (250 mL) of water with the sugar. Add the fennel, bring the water to a boil, turn down the heat, and simmer for 20 minutes, or until the fennel is tender. Set aside to cool in the syrup.

Preheat the oven to 350°F (180°C).

In a casserole dish (13- × 9-inch/33 × 23 cm), place the blueberries and fennel mixture, stir to mix, sprinkle with the tapioca starch, and stir well to mix again.

In a mixing bowl, combine the flour, brown sugar, and baking powder. Add the sour cream, butter, and lemon juice and zest. Stir until a smooth batter is formed. Spoon the batter onto the fennel and blueberries, leaving small gaps between spoonfuls. Place in the oven and bake for 40 minutes, or until the topping is browned and slightly puffy.

Serve warm with vanilla ice cream or whipped cream.

BEET AND APPLE CRUMBLE WITH MAPLE AND HAZELNUTS

Beets are earthy but also very sweet, and they pair well with the tart crispness of apple. Use boiled or baked beets cut into a fairly fine dice. You can use many types of oats for different results. Rolled oats give you a big flake with lots of crunch, steel cut oats give a firm texture, and instant oatmeal gives a softer texture. Any grade of maple syrup will work, though the lower grades are darker and will give more flavor—lighter syrups are more delicate and refined in flavor.

SERVES 8–10

1 cup (250 mL) rolled oats

1 cup (250 mL) all-purpose flour

½ cup (125 mL) chopped hazelnuts

1 cup (250 mL) melted butter

½ cup (125 mL) maple syrup

6 Fuji apples

1 cup (250 mL) diced cooked beets

¼ cup (65 mL) brown sugar

1 Tbsp (15 mL) tapioca starch
   (or cornstarch)

1 tsp (5 mL) ground cinnamon

1 tsp (5 mL) pure vanilla extract

Preheat the oven to 350°F (180°C).

In a mixing bowl, combine the oats, flour, hazelnuts, melted butter, and maple syrup. Stir well to combine.

Peel, core, and dice the apples then add them to a casserole dish (13- × 9-inch/33 × 23 cm) along with the cooked beets, brown sugar, tapioca, cinnamon, and vanilla. Stir well to mix. Top with the hazelnut crumble mixture and place it in the oven. Bake for 30 minutes, or until the topping is golden and the juices begin to bubble up on the edges of the crumble.

Serve warm with vanilla ice cream or whipped cream.

TOMATO AND BASIL PANNA COTTA

Tomato is actually a fruit, and when matched with honey and basil it creates a sweet, spicy, and mysterious flavor. You can also use 2 tablespoons (30 mL) agar-agar, a gelatin substitute made from seaweed, to substitute for the gelatin.

SERVES 4

1 cup (250 mL) milk

2 packages gelatin (2½ Tbsp/7 g each package)

2 cups (500 mL) whipping cream

1 cup (250 mL) tomato juice

½ cup (125 mL) honey

2 Tbsp (30 mL) chopped basil leaves

Whipped cream, for garnish

Sprig of mint or basil, for garnish

In a saucepan, place the milk and gelatin. Stir to dissolve, then warm through on medium-low heat for 5 minutes. Set aside for 5 minutes to steep.

Add the cream, tomato juice, honey, and basil. Bring to a boil, remove from the heat, and strain into a bowl or large measuring cup. Pour into four small ramekins, place them in a casserole dish, and allow to cool. Cover with plastic wrap and refrigerate for at least 4 hours, preferably overnight.

To serve, dip each ramekin into hot water and slide a sharp knife around the edge. Upturn on a dessert plate and shake to release the panna cotta. Garnish with a dollop of whipped cream and a sprig of mint and serve immediately.

PUMPKIN AND CANDIED GINGER PUDDING

This dessert is like a pumpkin pie pudding with its comforting texture and spices. Make sure the dessert has plenty of time to chill and set before serving.

SERVES 4–6

4 large egg yolks

1 cup (250 mL) brown sugar

¼ cup (65 mL) cornstarch

1 tsp (5 mL) ground cinnamon

¼ tsp (1 mL) freshly grated nutmeg

Pinch ground cloves

2 cups (500 mL) milk

2 cups (500 mL) whipping cream

2 cups (500 mL) pumpkin purée

1 Tbsp (15 mL) pure vanilla extract

2 Tbsp (30 mL) minced
   candied ginger

In a stand mixer fitted with a whisk attachment, combine the egg yolks with the sugar. Whisk until the yolks are pale and thick. While the machine is running, sprinkle in the cornstarch, cinnamon, nutmeg, and cloves. Whisk well to incorporate.

In a medium saucepan, heat the milk and cream until the mixture boils and doubles in volume. Remove from the heat and add the pumpkin purée. Bring back to a boil then pour one-third of the mixture into the egg yolks and stir with a hand-held whisk. Return the mixture to the saucepan and whisk to mix together all the ingredients. Add the vanilla, turn down the heat to low, and whisk until the mixture thickens.

Immediately remove from the heat, fold in the candied ginger, and transfer to ramekins or serving bowls. Place the dishes on a tray and allow to cool. Cover with plastic film and chill in the fridge for at least 4 hours, preferably overnight. Serve cold topped with fresh whipped cream.

CARAMELIZED CAULIFLOWER GRATIN

Cauliflower is an unusual choice for a dessert but the mild flesh is elevated by the addition of caramel. The topping is flavored with vanilla here, but another good choice would be a liqueur like Grand Marnier or limoncillo, or even sweet sherry.

SERVES 6–8

1 cauliflower, trimmed and cut
   into florets
1 cup (250 mL) granulated sugar
1 Tbsp (15 mL) butter
2 egg yolks
½ cup (125 mL) honey
2 cups (500 mL) whipping cream
1 tsp (5 mL) pure vanilla extract

Cook the cauliflower in a saucepan of boiling water for 2 to 3 minutes, or until barely tender. Drain and set aside until needed.

In a large sauté pan over high heat, combine the sugar with 1 cup (250 mL) of water. Bring to a boil, and then let the water evaporate until the sugar starts to brown on the edges. Swirl the pan to distribute the color. Add the butter and stir to mix. Add the drained cauliflower and toss to coat. Stir until the caramel is evenly distributed among the cauliflower. Transfer to a casserole dish (13- × 9-inch/ 33 × 23 cm) and set aside until needed.

In a mixing bowl, combine the egg yolks and honey. Whisk to mix well. In a saucepan over high heat, place the whipping cream and vanilla. Bring to a boil, remove immediately from the heat, and pour one-third of the mixture into the egg yolk mixture. Quickly stir with a rubber spatula to combine, return the mixture to the cream, and stir to mix. Return to low heat and stir with the spatula until the mixture thickens slightly (do not allow to boil). Remove from the heat and pour through a strainer over the cauliflower. Press with the spatula to force the cream through the sieve.

Set the broiler to high.

Place the gratin under the broiler and allow the top to bubble and brown. Remove from the heat and serve immediately.

PHYLLO ROLL WITH PARSNIP, WHITE CHOCOLATE, AND SESAME

White chocolate turns to caramel when baked between sheets of phyllo. Phyllo tends to dry out when exposed to air, so cover it with a clean, dry towel to prevent it from drying and splitting while you work. You could also use a purée of cauliflower with equally tasty results.

SERVES 4

2 cups (500 mL) cubed,
    peeled parsnip
2 cups (500 mL) chopped
    white chocolate
1 tsp (5 mL) pure vanilla extract
1 Tbsp (15 mL) butter
¼ cup (65 mL) honey
2 egg yolks
4 sheets phyllo pastry
¼ cup (65 mL) melted butter
½ cup (125 mL) grated
    white chocolate
1 Tbsp (15 mL) sesame seeds

In a saucepan, cover the parsnip with water. Bring to a boil, turn down the heat, and simmer for 10 minutes, or until the parsnip is tender. Drain and allow to sit in the sieve for a few minutes.

Place the chopped white chocolate in a bowl and microwave for 1 minute. Stir and microwave at 30-second intervals until melted and smooth. Return the parsnip to the saucepan and mash it with a potato masher (or fork). Add the melted chocolate and stir to mix. Add 1 tablespoon (15 mL) of butter and heat on low until the butter melts and the filling is hot and smooth. Add the honey and eggs yolks and stir to mix well. Remove from the heat and allow to cool to room temperature. Transfer this filling to a bowl and chill in the fridge for at least 1 hour.

Preheat the oven to 400°F.

Place a phyllo sheet on a clean work surface. Brush with some of the melted butter and sprinkle with one-quarter of the grated chocolate and sesame seeds. Fold over and brush this surface with butter. Place one-quarter of the filling on one end and fold over the edge to cover the filling. Form a tight log and roll to set the form of the log. Fold over the two ends and continue rolling into a tight log. Brush the last edge with a little more butter to seal the edge tightly. Place seam side down on a tray covered with parchment (silicon) paper and repeat with the remaining filling and phyllo. Chill for at least 15 minutes.

Brush the chilled rolls with a little more melted butter and place in the oven. Bake for 10 to 12 minutes, or until the pastry is browned and crisp. Transfer to serving plates and serve with vanilla ice cream or whipped cream.

CHOCOLATE, ORANGE, AND ZUCCHINI CAKE

Use a springform or Bundt cake pan for the best results. Butter the pan and dust it lightly with flour. If you like, you can cover the cake with a chocolate ganache. Melt 1 cup (250 mL) of chopped chocolate in ½ cup (125 mL) whipping cream. Whisk until smooth and then pour over the cake. Six ounces (170 g) of chocolate yields about 1 cup (250 mL) of chopped chocolate.

SERVES 6–8

½ cup (125 mL) butter
½ cup (125 mL) olive oil
1 cup (250 mL) granulated sugar
2 eggs
2 cups (500 mL) all-purpose flour
¼ cup (65 mL) cocoa powder
1 tsp (5 mL) baking powder
1 tsp (5 mL) salt
1 small orange, zest and juice
1 Tbsp (15 mL) Grand Marnier
1 tsp (5 mL) pure vanilla extract
2 cups (500 mL) shredded zucchini
6 oz (170 g) chopped dark chocolate

Preheat the oven to 350°F (180°C).

Grease and flour a 12-inch (3.5 L) springform cake pan. Set aside.

In a stand mixer fitted with a paddle attachment, combine the butter and olive oil. Add the sugar and whisk until fluffy. Add the eggs one at a time, beating well after each addition.

In a small bowl, combine the flour, cocoa powder, baking powder, and salt. Fold this into the eggs in three additions. When smooth, fold in the orange juice and zest, Grand Marnier, and vanilla with a whisk. Gently turn the mixture with a whisk until smooth, then fold in the zucchini and chocolate with a spatula.

Pour into the prepared cake pan and place on a baking tray. Place in the oven and bake for 35 to 40 minutes, or until a toothpick inserted in the centre comes out clean. Transfer to a wire rack and allow to cool to room temperature.

SPICED CARROT AND BEET CAKE

Beets add a depth of color to the cake along with an earthy sweetness. You could add a cream cheese icing to the cake, or glaze it with your favorite jam. I have used marmalade, apple butter, and quince jelly with excellent results.

SERVES 6–8

1 large beet, scrubbed

1 cup (250 mL) packed brown sugar

¾ cup (175 mL) vegetable oil

3 eggs

1 tsp (5 mL) pure vanilla extract

2 cups (500 mL) all-purpose flour

1 Tbsp (15 mL) baking powder

1 Tbsp (15 mL) ground cinnamon

1 Tbsp (15 mL) Five-Spice Powder
   (page 81)

1 tsp (5 mL) salt

2 cups (500 mL) shredded carrot

1 cup (250 mL) golden raisins

Preheat the oven to 350°F (180°C).

Grease and flour a 13- × 9-inch (33 × 23 cm) rectangle or 10-inch (25 cm) round metal cake pan. Set aside.

Place the beet on a rimmed baking tray and put in the oven. Bake for 30 minutes, or until tender. Remove from the oven and let cool to handling temperature. Peel the beet and rinse it under cold water. Grate the beet into a mixing bowl and set aside until needed.

In a stand mixer fitted with a paddle attachment, combine the sugar and oil. Add the eggs one at a time, beating well between additions. Add the vanilla and stir to mix.

In a small bowl, combine the flour, baking powder, cinnamon, Five-Spice Powder, and salt. Fold this into the batter in three additions. When smooth, fold in the grated beet, carrot, and raisins.

Pour the mixture into the prepared cake pan and place on a baking tray. Place in the hot oven and bake for 35 to 40 minutes, or until a toothpick inserted in the centre comes out clean. Transfer to a wire rack to cool. Turn out the cake onto a plate, glaze or ice it if you like, and cut it into squares.

INDEX

Edited by Lesley Cameron
Proofread by Claire Philipson
Cover and interior design by Pete Kohut
Food and interior photography by Bill Jones except,
pages ii–iii, ix, 50, 53–54, 104, 130 by Pete Kohut,
pages 62–63 by JoeRos, istockphoto.com,
page 87 by joannawnuk, istockphoto.com,
page 100 by ValentynVolkov, istockphoto.com,
page 115 by pilipphoto, istockphoto.com, and
page 240, by villagemoon, istockphoto.com.

Printed in China

Library and Archives Canada Cataloguing in Publication
Jones, W.A. (William Allen), 1959–, author
      The Deerholme vegetable cookbook / Bill Jones.

Issued in print and electronic formats.
ISBN 978-1-77151-129-2 (paperback).

      1. Cooking (Vegetables). 2. Cookbooks. I. Title.

TX801.J65 2015   641.6'5   C2015-904108-2

Canadian   Patrimoine
Heritage   canadien

The publisher acknowledges the financial support of the
Government of Canada through the Canada Book Fund
(CBF) and the Province of British Columbia through the
Book Publishing Tax Credit.

15 16 17 18 19   5 4 3 2 1

This book was produced using FSC®-certified, acid-free papers,
processed chlorine free, and printed with soya-based inks.